KEEP IT SIMPLE, MAKE IT BIG

KEEP IT
SIMPLE
MAKE IT
BIG

MONEY MANAGEMENT
FOR
A MEANINGFUL LIFE

**MICHAEL
LYNCH**

LIONCREST
PUBLISHING

KEEP IT SIMPLE, MAKE IT BIG
Money Management for a Meaningful Life

ISBN   978-1-5445-1553-3 *Hardcover*
         978-1-5445-1552-6 *Paperback*
         978-1-5445-1551-9 *Ebook*

To Tasha Blount, who puts the B in Team LB, and Micaela and Domenic, who, with Tasha's help, give me what I always wanted, a fun and happy home. To Mom and Dad, well, for everything.

CONTENTS

DISCLAIMER

This book is meant for educational purposes only. It's not intended to be personal financial advice for the simple reason that all situations are unique, and it is not written for you personally.

Michael Lynch is a registered representative of, and offers securities and investment advisory services through, MML Investors Services, LLC. Member SIPC. 6 Corporate Drive, Shelton, CT 06484

Representatives do not provide tax and/or legal advice. Any discussion of taxes is for general informational purposes only, does not purport to be complete or cover every situation, and should not be construed as legal, tax, or accounting advice. Clients should confer with their qualified legal, tax, and accounting advisors as appropriate.

All opinions expressed in this book are solely my opinions and do not reflect the opinions of my respective parent companies or affiliates or the companies with which I am affiliated.

Investments or strategies mentioned in this book may not be suitable for you, and you should make your own independent decision regarding them. This material does not take into account your particular investment objectives, financial situation, or needs and is not intended as recommendations appropriate for you. You should strongly consider seeking advice from your own investment adviser.

INTRODUCTION

This book was originally conceived of and designed to be a college-level introductory course to the exciting and complex field of personal financial management. Those looking for off-the-shelf answers to seemingly simple questions— What is the best way to save for retirement? Should I buy stocks or bonds? What mutual funds are the best? Should I buy term life insurance and invest the difference, or do I need permanent life insurance? Are variable annuities the best thing since air conditioning or the Devil's handiwork— won't find them here.

The answers to these questions are unique to each person. This book provides the framework, tools, and self-confidence to begin to answer these questions for yourself.

In some cases, the questions will be simple enough that this is all that's needed. In others, a person will gain enough knowledge to understand that professional help is needed. Most importantly, this book will equip you with a base of knowledge to ask the right questions and choose a course of action in an informed manner. As Socrates taught, asking the right question is the most important step to true knowledge. (He also taught that there's a time to quit asking, but that's another story.)

Although informed by the latest academic work, as well as insights from Aristotle to Yogi Berra, this work emerges from nearly two decades of financial planning experience with hundreds of American households—households ranging in income from under $30,000 annually to more than $3 million. This extensive experience taught me that there is no one right way for everyone to achieve financial success. There is a way for everyone to develop a plan that's right for them.

This book will empower you to design and implement strategies necessary for financial success as defined by enjoying a retirement free of financial worry, educating children and grandchildren, and making sure that no matter what life throws in your direction, you and the people you care about are never poor.

Michael Lynch CFP®

___

CHAPTER ONE

VISION AND VALUES

What does money mean to you? It's an important question, yet one that few people ask themselves. It's the first question I ask participants in a retirement-oriented class I teach. I've been helping people build, protect, use, and transfer wealth for nearly twenty years. I know that there are many answers and that each answer has important implications for how one designs a financial plan, an approach to life, and ultimately financial independence. Here are some common answers and approaches, although some may not be readily admitted.

- Freedom
- Security
- Time with family
- Power
- Control

Each of these is legitimate and each of them will lead to a slightly different approach to work, leisure, investing, and protecting wealth. A person who values freedom, for example, may place a premium on the spending side of financial life, keep a close eye on expenses, and invest a high proportion of after-tax income. This enables them to quit a job temporarily or even permanently, and not get boxed into bad situations. This is quite popular these days as the Financial Independence Retire Early (FIRE) movement demonstrates. How they invest their savings will depend on their overall risk preferences and ability to tolerate the downs of ownership investments. But they better have a plan to stay independent and therefore free.

A person who values the power that money provides—and it can provide a lot—will have a different relationship to work, spending, and investing. For most, work is the source of at least some power and plenty of income that facilitates spending, which itself provides both real and perceived power. Someone who values the power of money will likely work longer, save and invest much less, and consume a higher portion of income. These choices will drive a need to work longer to support the lifestyle. How this person saves and invests will again be driven by many factors, but the need for consumption will require a commensurate need for near-term liquidity to pay the bills.

The second question I often ask is simple:

What is your ideal retirement?

This question often elicits some blank stares, so I follow it up with specifics that assist people in moving through their checklists.

Where are you living?

- Your current home
- Condo in Florida
- Trailer in Mexico
- Hacienda in Spain
- House in California
- Apartment in Greenwich Village

What are you doing?

- Working at Walmart
- Volunteering at church, temple, or synagogue
- Tending your garden
- Surfing in San Diego
- Taking care of grandchildren
- Traveling the country in a motor coach

Where is your money coming from?

- Social Security
- Employer-sponsored pension

- IRA
- Tax-deferred annuity
- Personal investments
- Part-time income
- Children

This last bullet produces laughter and rolling eyes. I know this as I have been one of those children who at times caused the money to move in the wrong direction—from parent to child.

Setting aside us deadbeat children for a moment, these big questions are exactly what this book is designed to assist you in fleshing out. It won't provide you the answers, but it will allow you to frame the questions in ways that are meaningful to you and your loved ones and provide your own answers. For areas where you feel you need professional help, it will educate you to be an informed consumer of financial services and perhaps even a great client for some lucky advisor.

This book is retirement oriented. All things must have a focus, so retirement it is. That said, many of the discussions will apply to life's other great financial goals and stages—accumulating for education for children, for example. From cover to cover, this book will help you:

- Begin the process of dreaming the big dreams required to define your retirement goals
- Understand the resources you will need to accumulate to realize your dreams
- Help you amass more resources by paying less in taxes
- Develop a robust system to turn accumulated assets into useful income
- Manage life's risks so that you drastically reduce your chances of being poor or dependent on your children or the government
- Transfer your assets to your children, not to Congress and the state legislatures
- Put it all together in a plan for your future—which, after all, starts today

SIMPLE STEPS TO MAKE IT BIG

- Set aside time with your spouse, loved ones, or just yourself to brainstorm your future.
- Bring yellow pads and ask yourself and each other the questions in this chapter.
- Don't prejudge. Big goals motivate. Don't ask, "Why?" Ask, "Why not?"

CHAPTER TWO

BYPASSING THE ROADBLOCKS

Begin at the beginning and go on 'til you come to the end; then stop.

—LEWIS CARROLL

This is not your grandparents' retirement.

It promises to last far longer. A baby boy born in 1935, the year Social Security was founded, could expect to live sixty years, seven short of the time needed to collect a check. A baby girl was expected to survive until 64.[1] Back then, Social Security really did address the "risk" of living a long life.

---

1   Elizabeth Arias, PhD, and Jiaquan Xu, MD, "United States Life Tables, 2015," National Vital Statistics Reports, Volume 67, Number 7, Table 19.

A baby boy born in 2015 can expect to live until 78. A baby girl is projected to reach 81.[2] Today, if a couple both reach 65, one person can expect to live until age 93. There's a one in four chance that one will live until 97.[3]

This couple, if both call it quits at 65, needs a plan to generate real, inflation-adjusted income for thirty years!

Longevity is the reality we all face. On balance, this is a good thing, of course, but all silver linings have clouds. I recall my grandfather's quip, "If I knew I was going to live so long, I would have taken better care of myself."

The question you must ask: Am I prepared to finance a thirty-year retirement? How much should I "take care of" my finances to make these years financially healthy?

Shockingly, many don't think they need to take such care. Nearly one in two Americans expects to be retired for fewer than twenty years. Sixteen percent expect to live less than fifteen years after saying goodbye to paid employment.[4] A recent survey found that more than half of respondents had no idea how long they'd live. This is the most accurate

---

2   Ibid.

3   Joint life expectancy tables published on Financial Architects webpage, accessed February 10, 2019, www.financialarcitectsllc.com.

4   ING Retirement Readiness & Middle America Survey, 2004, Prepared by KRC Research.

response.[5] It also dives directly to the core of the problem: planning in the face of uncertainty. After you've pondered your longevity, ask yourself this: Is the government prepared to finance your retirement for thirty years?

You'll probably come up with, *Well, maybe.* Its two main programs for middle-class support are Social Security and Medicare. Each is struggling with its own issues of aging. According to the 2018 Annual Report of the Social Security Trustees:

> Cost is projected to exceed projected income throughout the projection period...To illustrate the magnitude of the 75-year actuarial deficit, consider that for the combined OASI and DI Trust Funds to remain fully solvent throughout the 75-year projection period: (1) revenues would have to increase by an amount equivalent to an immediate and permanent payroll tax rate increase of 2.78 percentage points to 15.18 percent, (2) scheduled benefits would have to be reduced by an amount equivalent to an immediate and permanent reduction of about 17 percent applied to all current and future beneficiaries, or about 21 percent if the reductions were applied only to those who become initially eligible for benefits in 2018 or later; or (3) some combination of these approaches would have to be adopted.[6]

---

5   "A Precarious Existence: How Today's Retirees Are Financially Faring in Retirement," Transamerica Center for Retirement Studies, December 2018, p. 4.

6   The 2018 Annual Report of the Board of Trustees of the Old-Age Survivors Insurance and Federal Disability Trust Funds.

Bottom line, if no action is taken—and there's nothing pending—the trustees project a nearly 25 percent reduction in benefits will be required in 2034.

Are you prepared for a 25-percent cut in pay?

You need a plan if Uncle Sam uses any of the strategies available to erode the real value of your Social Security.

When I changed careers from professional writing and advising people on personal finance as a hobby to professional financial advising and writing as a hobby, my mother sent me an editorial cartoon depicting a squirrel couple who'd brought their nuts to a financial advisor. The caption: "If you take a late retirement and an early death, you just may make it."

Don't let this be your script.

To avoid this fate, you must understand and avoid the roadblocks that prevent financial success. In fact, you must execute financial jiu jitsu, turning the power of the roadblock into your strength. These roadblocks are:

- Taxes
- Not saving enough
- Inflation
- Taking too much risk

- Not taking enough risk
- Unexpected human problems
- Procrastination
- Failing to plan

ROADBLOCK 1: TAXES

I like to pay taxes. With them I buy civilization.

—OLIVER WENDELL HOLMES JR.

I'm proud to pay taxes in the United States; the only thing is, I could be just as proud for half the money.

—ARTHUR GODFREY

To state the obvious, you don't want to overpay for civilization.

Taxes are certainly unavoidable and necessary, they do purchase many great things, and this is not an anti-tax or anti-government screed. This section is merely designed to point out that our tax system is called a "code" for a reason. It does offer us many choices on when and under what conditions we pay our fair share of taxes. If we choose wisely, our fair share may just be a little bit less than if we stayed on automatic pilot.

Ponder this: When would you prefer to pay your taxes: now, later, or never? To help answer this, consider you invest

$100,000, earn 7 percent annual return, and face a 27 percent combined marginal income tax rate (22 percent federal plus 5 percent state).

The never-taxed option is of course the best, and it's no surprise that, like red wine, it gets better the longer one delays. If you are never taxed, after twenty years, the initial investment has nearly quadrupled to $386,968. The person who deferred taxes for later but must settle up after twenty years will have $309,487. If you pay taxes along the way, you will accumulate $270,945.

So, the order is an easy-to-grasp hierarchy. Never is best, followed by later. The last option is pay along the way.

If we change the assumptions, this clarity gets cloudy. The higher the tax rates, the more value in deferring taxes. Yet many people move down brackets at various points in their lives. In these years, pay as you go may be the way to go.

Taxable investment accounts, for example, are currently nearly tax-free for people in the 10- and 12-percent federal tax brackets. The rate on dividends and capital gains is zero. That's right. Zero! That's my favorite tax bracket.

Standard advice proffered by gurus is maximize pre-tax accounts prior to using other investments. This is often wrong given today's tax code, a financial version of the medieval bloodletting to restore a patient strength. Now, as back then, it can kill the patient.

Consider the fate of a college graduate who elects the pre-tax option on his first employer's retirement plan. Given his starting salary, he defers taxes at less than 15 percent, saving a mere $150 for every $1,000 he invests. Yet when it comes time to withdraw, he pays double the tax on the way out due to his higher income.

One of personal finance's great ironies is that while we're working, we love pre-tax retirement plans, as they save us taxes, and we dislike taxable investments, as they generate money for Uncle Sam. Once retired, however, the roles are reversed. Retirement plans generate taxes—and may force us to pay more for our Medicare premiums—while taxable accounts are far more tax friendly.

It's called the tax "code" for a reason. Taking time to crack the code and apply it to your personal situation can save you thousands of dollars in unnecessary taxes. If you feel guilty for outsmarting the system and not paying enough, you can always send extra to Uncle Sam and your state capitol. I doubt you will, however, as a charity will likely be a better choice.

ROADBLOCK 2: NOT SAVING ENOUGH, SPENDING TOO MUCH

It's easier to spend $2 than it is to save $1.

—WOODY ALLEN

You must break the law to retire comfortably—Parkinson's Law. Cyril Northcote Parkinson, a British historian, stated "Work expands to fill the time available for its completion."[7] The financial translation: one's expenses expand to consume all available income.

Break the law! Drive a wedge between income and expenses. In your working years, set a goal to save 10 to 20 percent of your income. You can start low and increase percentage every year at annual increase time. Pay yourself now and later at the same time.

The ease of execution fluctuates with the stages of life.

When we are young and starting out, it is often our easiest time to drive this wedge and create the habit of saving. This is why I love working with young people. After all, bad habits are hard to develop but easy to live with. Good habits are harder to develop, but much easier to live with. Saving and investing a significant portion of income is just such a habit.

---

7   Attributed to British Historian Cyril Northcote Parkinson (1909-1993). The American Heritage Dictionary, accessed December 17, 2004, http://www.bartleby.com/61/54/P0075400.html.

I often pull out my financial calculator to show astonished parents that if their just-graduated child invests 10 percent of their $50,000 starting salary for ten years and never invests another dime after a decade, then this alone is enough to provide for the non-Social Security portion of retirement.

Many of us move from lower income but lower obligation 20s and early 30s, to the higher income but much higher obligation mid-30s, 40s, and early 50s. By then, many of us have made life's great mistakes: marriage, homeownership, and children.

Okay, that's a joke.

These are life's great joys, perhaps, but they crimp cash flow and cost a lot of money. In this phase, retirement investing may transition to education financing, home payments, family vacations, and extracurricular activities. This is usually okay provided one saves in their early stages.

By the time people make it into my retirement classes, most are exiting this stage into the final run to pre-retirement. Now the financial stars are realigning for success: peak earnings, children's education in rearview mirror, and children mostly on their own. In this phase, it's critical to do some planning, determine accumulation needs for retirement income, and redirect money that was going to children and housing to your retirement. Everyone's journey is unique, of course. That's why it's key to customize your plan.

Regardless of which phase you find yourself at present, the basics remain the same.

The best way to save more money is to spend less. A person paying 30 percent marginal taxes must earn $1.43 to spend $1. This is brutal math.

That $3.00 latte costs $4.29. For a person earning $50,000 a year, that's fifteen minutes of work. Is it worth it? For some, the answer is absolutely. For others, no way.

It's important to create systems that fit your personality. Finance is a lot like fitness: it only works when applied consistently over many years. I, for example, hate exercising in the morning. I prefer a cup of coffee, a good read or a writing project. It's my creative time. So, if I design a morning exercise routine, I will not stick with it. I work out in late afternoon, usually with my children. I can stick to that.

In financial terms, know what kind of saver you are: Type A or Type B.

Type A savers pay monthly bills and invest what's left over. The key is with Type A's there is something left to invest.

Type B savers pay monthly bills and invest what's left. The problem is that there's nothing left!

Type B savers, most of whom have never been a day late on a single bill in their life, need to give themselves two new types of bills.

The first is bills that will build up wealth over time. These include 401(k) deductions from a paycheck and automatic investment withdrawals from bank accounts to such things as Roth IRAs, college, and non-qualified investment accounts.

The second types of bills are those that will make sure they are never poor. These include systematic life and disability insurance premiums, some of which will also build wealth.

Most of us are Type B's. If this is you, don't delay setting up an automatic wealth creation and protection program.

THE PROBLEM OF CREDIT

While on the topic of spending, here's an idea: don't abuse credit!

Notice I didn't say, "Don't use credit." There is nothing wrong with credit per se. It's simply a tool that, like any other, such as dynamite, can be employed to build wonderful things or destroy wonderful things. Some credit is excellent, and some is disastrous.

Now when I'm talking about credit, I'm talking about running a balance and paying interest. I see smart people do this all the time. Ten thousand on a card at 18 percent costs $150 a month in interest. That is enough to fund a great date night. Yet, even people who pay the card off each month should be careful about what they use to purchase life's necessities.

A study that focused on how much people would pay for basketball tickets found that individuals who were paying by credit card were willing to spend twice as much as those paying with cash![8] This makes sense, as it's harder to pull a wad of $20s from the wallet than to swipe a card. Why do you think merchants are willing to pay credit card companies 3 percent of each purchase we make on plastic? Ultimately it all comes from our paychecks. Credit cards offer users many benefits, just make sure that you are not overpaying for them. Let someone else provide the profits.

Ask yourself, what am I financing?

Is it an appreciating asset such as a home or education? Is it a necessary input to build wealth such as a car or perhaps

---

8   Gary Belsky and Thomas Gilovich, "Why Smart People Make Big Money Mistakes and How to Correct Them: Lessons from the New Science of Behavioral Economics," 1999, p. 43.

a professional wardrobe? Or, is it a consumption item such as a vacation or dinner out that ought to be purchased with income left over after investments have been made?

ROADBLOCK 3: THE CORROSIVE EFFECTS OF INFLATION

Ever consider why being on a "fixed income" is often referred to negatively? Most people, after all, prefer a fixed income to a variable income. The reason is that in the retirement context, a portion of the income is often fixed—level pension, income from bonds or CDs—while life's expenses climb relentlessly. Even at modest rates, inflation destroys the purchasing power of the dollar over long periods of time.

For a thirty-year retirement, if inflation runs at the recent five-year trendline of 1.86 percent, $1 the day you retire will be worth only $0.58 your last year of retirement. If prices increase the thirty-year average of 3.13 percent, it will be worth $0.40. If the Federal Reserve achieves its target of 2 percent, $1 will be worth a mere $0.55 in thirty years, cutting the value of a fixed-income payment such as an annuity income or corporate pension in half.

Inflation likely will be greater for the retired you than the working you. Retirees tend to purchase more services as they age, such as healthcare, and need to consume basics such as energy and utilities that are excluded from the standard index used to calculate inflation. These tend to increase at a greater inflation rate than many other products, as the main cost is US labor.[9]

The Bureau of Labor Statistics created a more realistic index that weighted basics such as healthcare more heavily and included energy. It found that inflation was 8 percent higher than standard reporting.[10] Healthcare prices alone increased at three times the general inflation rate, from 2013 to 2018, according to one study.[11] The cost of fuels and utilities for consumers jumped 87 percent from 2000 through 2018.[12]

These relentless price escalations require people to allocate a portion of their savings to investments that beat inflation. These tend to be considered "risky," as what goes up also goes down. For safety, these investments need to be embedded in an integrated plan to offset fixed-income

9   "The Gap Between Services Inflation and Goods Inflation," The Federal Reserve Bank of Cleveland, June 2, 2015, accessed February 20, 2019, https://www.clevelandfed.org/newsroom-and-events/publications/economic-trends/2015-economic-trends/et-20150602-the-gap-between-services-inflation-and-goods-inflation.aspx.

10 Jonathan Church, "The Cost of 'Basic Necessities' Has Risen Slightly More Than Inflation over the Last 30 Years," Bureau of Labor Statistics, Beyond the Numbers, June 2015, Vol. 4, No. 10, accessed February 10, 2019, https://www.bls.gov/opub/btn/volume-4/the-cost-of-basic-necessities-has-risen-slightly-more-than-inflation-over-the-last-30-years.htm.

11 Alex Kacik, "Healthcare price growth significantly outpaces inflation," Modern Healthcare, October 25, 2018. https://www.modernhealthcare.com/article/20181025/NEWS/181029946 Accessed February 10, 2019.

12 Federal Reserve Bank of St. Louis, "Consumer Price Index for all Urban Consumers: Fuels and Utilities," https://fred.stlouisfed.org/series/CUUR0000SAH2 Accessed February 10, 2019.

investments. How safe, after all, are investments that are designed to depreciate over time?

Finally, unexpected expenses, a unique form of inflation, must also be considered. My retired clients often face unexpected bills of $5,000 to $10,000 for such one-time items as hearing aids, dental work, and home and car repairs. Teeth and ears are expensive. Medicare doesn't pay for them. Years of research shows that life with teeth and hearing is better than a life without them. You will pay for them, so it's best to plan for it.

ROADBLOCK 4: TAKING TOO MUCH INVESTMENT RISK

Like it or not, modern American economic life makes investors out of most of us. Starting with the introduction of IRAs in 1974 and accelerating with the 401(k) in 1980, retirement has slowly shifted from being the province of large organizations working on our behalf to being our responsibility. The good news is that we have far more tools and options than did previous generations. There has been an explosion of mutual funds, many targeted to specific retirement dates, Roth accounts, after-tax and pre-tax options. All this can be overwhelming and often is. The result is these three mistakes:

- Speculating instead of investing
- Failure to allocate investments over many asset classes
- Failure to diversify investments within asset classes

Concentration of company stock in a 401(k) plan is an all-too-common mistake. At Enron, a famous corporate blowup in 2001, 62 percent of the assets in employee self-directed 401(k) accounts was Enron stock. Eighty-nine percent of this stock was purchased by employees.[13]

When Enron's stock became worthless, so did 62 percent of the account balances in Enron employees' 401(k)s. The pain was real and irrevocable. "I can tell you, without pulling punches, that something stinks here," 63-year-old Charles Prestwood told a Senate committee. Prestwood retired from Enron and had 99 percent of his $1.3 million 401(k) balance in company stock. "I lost everything I had."[14]

Enron is no aberration. It was not the first company stock calamity and it won't be the last. Employees at companies such as Merck, WorldCom, and RiteAid have experienced sharp declines in values as well.

Enron did scare many straight. At that time, company stock accounted for 16 percent of 401(k) assets. Today it is down to 10 percent. This understates the effective concentration since not all companies offer stock options in their 401(k).

Government regulations limit companies from having more

---

13 Patrick J. Purcell, "The Enron Bankruptcy and Employer Stock in Retirement Plans," CRS Report for Congress, updated March 11, 2002.

14 David Ivanovich, "Enron's 401(k) Claims Disputed," *Houston Chronicle*, January 17, 2002.

than 10 percent of company stock in their defined-benefit pensions.[15] There's a good reason for this and experts suggest that individuals ought to heed it, but many don't. As of 2016, employees at many large companies remained concentrated in employer stock.[16]

A stock doesn't have to become worthless to punish over-concentrated investors. As recently as 2016, roughly one in three dollars in General Electric's 401(k) plan was in company stock.[17] From 2009 to 2019, the value of this stock languished between $8.75 a share and $7.75 at the end, a lost decade.[18] The diversified S&P tripled over the same period.[19]

ROADBLOCK 5: NOT TAKING ENOUGH INVESTMENT RISK

You face two real investment risks in retirement. First, you can permanently lose the money you invested. Notice I said

15 Patrick J. Purcell, "The Enron Bankruptcy and Employer Stock in Retirement Plans," CRS Report for Congress, updated March 11, 2002, 29 U.S.C. ~1107(a).

16 Robert C. Pozen and Ming Liu, "Having Too Much Employer Stock in Your 401(k) Is Dangerous. Just Look at GE," Brookings Institution, July 3, 2018, accessed February 16, 2019, https://www.brookings.edu/opinions/having-too-much-employer-stock-in-your-401k-is-dangerous-just-look-at-ge/. Originally appeared in Fortune, June 20, 2018.

17 "Column: Beyond GE-U.S. Workers Own Too much Company Stock in Retirement Plans," Reuters Wealth, July 12, 2008, accessed February 16, 2019, https://www.reuters.com/article/us-column-miller-employerstock/column-beyond-ge-u-s-workers-own-too-much-company-stock-in-retirement-plans-idUSKBN1K234Z.

18 Price data from Macrotrends, accessed February 16, 2019, https://www.macrotrends.net/stocks/charts/GE/general-electric/stock-price-history.

19 S&P 500 Historical Prices by Year, accessed February 16, 2019, http://www.multpl.com/s-p-500-historical-prices/table/by-year.

"permanently," as in you invested in a dot.com company and it went bust. This is what Enron employees experienced. It can be devastating. It is also easy to avoid.

The second risk is losing the value of your invested money to inflation. This, like carbon monoxide poisoning, is a slow, hard-to-detect process that does not end well.

I often say that termites do more damage than hurricanes. Hurricanes are company collapses. Termites are inflation.

Each person must find his or her own balance between these two risks. The danger, however, is to overemphasize the risk of losing money while underemphasizing the risk of the erosion of purchasing power.

Playing it too safe guarantees one thing: you'll lose money safely. If people define safety as something that can't lose value, they limit their investment options to government bonds and bank and insurance products such as CDs, money markets, and fixed annuities. These play important roles in most financial plans, but when they play the dominant role, the actual risk is that real, after-tax returns will lag inflation and people will be forced to invade principal. This is especially true in retirement plans that must be drawn down starting at age 72 at a rough rate of 3.6 percent. And this rate increases with a person's age.

I always advise clients to look back to look forward. Do you know anyone who paid more for their last car than their first house?

That's inflation.

What did a breakfast at a diner cost you twenty years ago? What does it cost today?

That's inflation.

Were you happy with your paycheck twenty years ago? Would you be happy with the same paycheck today?

That's inflation.

I then ask about the last financial crisis.

How much did your accounts go down? Faces grimace. How long did it take you to get to even? The frowns start to turn around.

What is the value of that account today, a decade later? In most cases, its value has exploded. And it's here that understanding appears.

Classical Philosophy provides insight to the balancing of

risks with Aristotle's Golden Mean, commonly defined as "Not too little, not too much, but just enough."

Another way to frame the balance between risk and security is all virtue is found between two vices. Courage, for example, is certainly a virtue. It is the golden mean between the vices of Cowardice and Foolhardiness.

The key is to find your "golden mean" of investing.

Over a twenty-year period, stock market investors, with dividends reinvested, have never lost money. The risk of losing the actual dollars a person invests diminishes with time and historically always drops to zero—*eventually*.

In fact, the income potential of diversified US stocks as expressed in the S&P 500 index whips inflation and produces an increasing income. Over the last twenty years, from 1999 through 2018,

- The consumer price index increased by 53 percent.
- Cash dividends from the S&P 500 increased by 230 percent.
- The actual value of the index increased by just over 100 percent.

In other words, inflation went up by 1.6X, the value of the index increased by 2X and the income increased by

3.3X.[20] A couple who hitched their financial wagon to this horse actually more than doubled both their real income and net worth in retirement.

ROADBLOCK 6: THE THREE D'S: DISABILITY, DEATH, AND DIVORCE

Life brings both unexpected sorrows as well as its share of joys. They can't be predicted but they can be planned for.

Shockingly, one in three people under age 35 will experience a disability during his or her career.[21] One in two of those people will still be disabled five years later.[22] Unless supplemented with private action, the default income source will be the government: Social Security disability for the long-term disabled. The average monthly check from Social Security Disability Income is $1,198.[23] Will you be able to live on this? Who pays the mortgage? Who funds the retirement plan?

The average American who has life insurance has 3.4 times his or her salary in a group term plan.[24] I often ask people,

20   Calculations from political calculations, accessed August 24, 2019.

21   1985 Society of Actuaries Commissioner Report.

22   Ibid.

23   Social Security Administration, Annual Statistical Report on the Social Security Disability Insurance Program, 2017.

24   Facts About Life 2017, Facts from LIMRA Life Insurance Awareness Month, September 2017, accessed February 16, 2019, https://www.limra.com/uploadedFiles/limra.com/LIMRA_Root/Posts/PR/LIAM/PDF/Facts-of-Life_2017(1).pdf.

"How long do you plan on being dead?" It gets a laugh and drives home the point that if this is all the protection people have, most families who lose a breadwinner can expect to suffer a significant decline in standard of living. Research supports this. A study at Boston University found that a quarter of families would suffer at least a 20 percent drop in their standard of living if the primary earner died.[25]

These perils are not limited to the young. One in six Americans in the final stretch of work, those ages 51 to 61, saw their retirement plans disrupted by a disability, divorce, or death of a spouse.[26]

Increasingly retirees are facing the high costs of long-term custodial care—$82,608 a year for the national average and much higher in the Northeast where many of my clients reside—should they require assistance in completing the activities of daily living.[27] I call this paying rent in the wrong kind of hotel. The government will pick up the tab eventually, but only after a person is impoverished.

---

25 B. Douglas Bernheim, Solange Berstein, Jagadeesh Gokhale, and Laurence Kotlikoff, "Saving and Life Insurance Holdngs at Boston University—A Unique Case Study," May 2002.

26 John B. Williamson and Tay K. McNamara, "The Effect of Unplanned Events on Retirement," Prepared for the Fifth Annual Joint Conference on Retirement Research Consortium, "Securing Retirement Income for Tomorrow's Retirees," May 15–16, 2003.

27 U.S. Administration on Aging, accessed February 16, 2019, https://longtermcare.acl.gov/costs-how-to-pay/costs-of-care.html.

ROADBLOCK 7: PROCRASTINATION AND DELAY.

You may delay, but time will not, and lost time is never found again.

—BENJAMIN FRANKLIN

Sally and Sue, a loving pair of twins, graduate from college and get their first jobs at 22.

Sally signs up for her employer's 401(k) plan and figures she can afford $200 a month, or $2,400 a year. As a bonus, she's told it lowers her taxes. She contributes for ten years, at which time she has two children, an expensive mortgage, day care, and she can no longer afford the contribution. She lets the money sit, earning an average of 10 percent annually, which she reinvests. At retirement, her investment of $24,000 has turned into $1.2 million.

Sue feels she has better uses for her money. She's young, after all, and retirement is far, far away. She can't recall what she's spent her money on, but at 32 she knows she'd better start saving for retirement. Although she's earning more, she too has the expenses associated with a growing family. She puts $200 a month into her 401(k), where it also compounds at 10 percent annually. At 67, her full retirement age, she has $685,000, or 43 percent less money than Sally. Worse, she contributed more than three times as much as her sister!

The best time for you to get started might have been a decade back. But the next best time is today. There's a reason the windshield is so much bigger than the rearview mirror. Focus forward as that's where you will spend the rest of your life. I have seen tremendous levels of wealth accumulated in the decade prior to retirement. Remember, your time horizon is not the ten years until you retire, but forty years until you move on to what's next.

ROADBLOCK 8: FAILING TO PLAN

You've got to be very careful if you don't know where you're going, because you might not get there.

—YOGI BERRA

Americans spend more time planning for vacations than planning for retirement.[28]

Don't rely on rules of thumb, such as, "You need $1 million in your 401(k)," "You will need only 70 percent of your income in retirement," "You won't need life insurance after you retire." You are unique. Your situation is unique. The price of failure is too high.

Go back to the basics and ask yourself the important questions:

---

28 2003 Employee Benefit Research Institute Retirement Confidence Survey.

- What's your ideal retirement?
- Will you be moving or staying put? This will determine state income tax rates, a potentially large expense or savings in retirement.
- Downsizing or upsizing? After taxes, housing is often the largest expense. Will yours be increasing or decreasing? Either is possible.
- Traveling the world or tending to your garden? Some of my clients spend substantial money on travel in retirement. Others have been there, done that, and prefer to stay put and enjoy their front porch. This has financial implications.
- How much will it cost? Put all this together, and you can figure out an annual price tag for your desired retired life.

Once you've done this, it's time to act.

- What steps can you take today to move in the optimal direction? Downsize your house, increase savings, track a budget, evaluate your investments.
- What risks must you manage to ensure that you and your family are not derailed?
- Are you dependent on the next decade of earnings from yourself or a spouse? If so, you will want to pay special attention to the risks of disability and death.

If you need help with the calculations or desire a partner, get professional help.

There are plenty of resources for people who want to do the heavy lifting themselves. For those who want a professional partner, we are here to help.

SIMPLE STEPS TO MAKE IT BIG

- Determine which roadblocks are affecting you.
- Determine the portion of your pre-tax income you are setting aside for the future.
- Stop procrastinating, and determine whether you will be your sole planner or would benefit from professional help.

CHAPTER THREE

CREATING YOUR OWN PAYCHECK IN RETIREMENT

WHERE'S IT GOING TO COME FROM AND HOW MUCH WILL YOU NEED?

[W]orker confidence in having enough money to retire comfortably seems to remain unrelated to whatever economic conditions exist....Almost half of workers (47 percent) who have not saved for retirement are at least somewhat confident about having enough money in retirement, with expectations that their retirement money will inevitably come from somewhere. America appears to be a nation of optimists when it comes to retirement, but for some people the Retirement dream may turn into a nightmare.

—DALLAS SALISBURY, PRESIDENT AND CEO OF
EMPLOYEE BENEFIT RESEARCH INSTITUTE[29]

29   Press release for EBRI's 2004 Retirement Confidence Survey.

This stunning quote illustrates a point I've experienced many times in nearly two decades working face-to-face with Americans. There is an inverse relationship between one's confidence in achieving financial independence and the probability that it will occur.

Let's examine some expectations versus reality that have been persistently stubborn for some time.

When asked what will drive income in retirement, Americans place personal investments at nearly 50 percent, or providing $1 out of every $2 spent. In reality, investments only generate $1 in $10. Oops. Interestingly, people pick pensions and Social Security just about spot on.[30]

And we are not just wrong about our investments. Americans plan to work longer than statistics show we actually do. The average person plans to retire at 65. The average retiree, however, calls it quits at 62.[31] That's three fewer years of earnings and savings and three more years of withdrawals and depletions. Nearly one in two American workers was forced to quit working earlier than they had planned. Forty percent did so due to disability or health problem. A quarter

30 U.S. Department of Social Services Administration on Aging and Administration Community Living, "2017 Profile of Older Americans," accessed February 16, 2019. https://acl.gov/sites/default/files/Aging%20and%20Disability%20in%20America/2017OlderAmericansProfile.pdf. And press release for EBRI's 2004 Retirement Confidence Survey.

31 2018 RCS Fact Sheet #2 Expectations about Retirement," EBRI, accessed February 16, 2019, https://www.ebri.org/docs/default-source/rcs/6_rcs_18-fs-2_expect.pdf?sfvrsn=e1e9302f_2.

did so due to changes at their employer.[32] At best, a mere 35 percent left on their own terms.

Four out of five Americans say they will continue to work part-time in retirement. Reasons given include health insurance benefits, needing the money to purchase life's essentials, wanting the money for life's extras, or enjoying work.

The reality is that far fewer will be able to work in retirement than plan to do so. Although four in five expect to work in retirement, a mere one in three suit up and get to work.

Don't be a negative statistic. You need a plan. In retirement, most people transition from an employee working for someone else to CEO of their very own retirement corporation. Being the boss means that you, not someone else, are responsible for making payroll.

PIECING TOGETHER YOUR PAYCHECK: SOURCES OF INCOME IN RETIREMENT OTHER THAN WORKING

So what is your plan to piece together your retirement income? Here's your menu of options:

- Social Security
- Defined-benefit pension

---

32   Ibid.

- Defined-contribution pension
- Other personal savings
- Inheritance
- Charity, family, and others

Let's examine each to build the optimal three-legged stool.

SOCIAL SECURITY: LEG ONE ON A THREE-LEGGED STOOL

Social Security is a government-sponsored defined-benefit pension. In addition to its retirement benefits, Social Security also offers protection for disabled workers (government-sponsored disability insurance) and widows and orphans (government-sponsored life insurance). Although it's sponsored by the government, it's paid for by workers who pay taxes on wages during their lifetimes. The 2020 tax rates are 12.4 percent on income up to $137,700, half of which is paid for directly by the employee and the other half paid directly by the employer.

To qualify for benefits, a person must pay into the system for forty quarters, or ten years, or be attached to someone who has. Benefits are calculated as a percentage of a worker's average annual wage over a thirty-five-year period, with a cap on how much can be paid out. The average benefit paid in 2020 is $1,503 a month. The maximum at full retirement age is $3,011 a month. The 2020 maximum benefit is $3,790 per month for a person who waits until 70 to collect.

The program is designed to replace 40 percent of the average worker's wage prior to full retirement age. It replaces much less for high earners. At the peak earning of $137,700, it replaces 26 percent at full retirement age.

The question to ask: Can you live on 40 percent of my average wage? If you are a six-figure earner, can you live on 25 percent or even less?

You also face the burden of deciding when to collect your benefits. When you collect determines what you get. Originally, Americans were eligible for full benefits at age 65. To shore up the system's finances, the full retirement age has been increased based on birth year and tops out at 67 for those born after 1960. It's 66 for those born between 1943 and 1954, and it phases up for those born between 1954 and 1960.

Workers are eligible for reduced benefits at age 62. Benefits are permanently reduced by an assigned percentage for each year benefit is taken before full retirement age. For those fully eligible at age 67, it's nearly a third lower.

For example, a person with a full benefit of $2,500 at age 67 will collect $1,750 at 62. That's a permanent reduction. There's a substantial penalty for early withdrawal!

The flip side of being punished for retiring early is that the government will pay you to wait. For those born after 1960, the benefit at age 70 will be 124 percent of the full retirement benefit you would get at 67, and 154 percent of the benefit you could have claimed at age 62.

So by waiting until age 70, a person can turn the $2,500 into $3,100 a month. This is a good strategy, unless this person checks out before 80.

Don't delay past 70, however, as that's the last year you'll enjoy an increase.

SHOULD I TAKE EARLY SOCIAL SECURITY?

The answer, as usual, is that it depends on your plan. As a rule, a person must live ten to twelve years from commencing benefits to break even. That is, a person who waits from 62 to 66 will be better off if she lives until age 78. Since life expectancy at age 70 is 14.3 years for men and 16.44 for women, on average, there is value in waiting.[33]

It's a complicated system with a labyrinth of intersecting rules. There is no one solution that applies to all. It pays to apply the rules to your unique situation.

---

33   Social Security Administration Actuarial Life Table, accessed February 16, 2019, https://www.ssa.gov/oact/STATS/table4c6.html.

Questions to ask yourself: How long do I expect to live? How long have others in my family lived? How much do I need the Social Security income?

Don't forget the rules. You may not be able to collect early even if you desire to do so. If you expect to have significant earned income in retirement—more than $1,470 a month or $17,640 in 2019—the answer is probably not, since the heavy penalty imposed on your Social Security benefit would substantially reduce or eliminate the real value of earnings. The penalty is $1 for every $2 earned over the limit. In the year a person reaches full retirement age, they can earn up to $3,910 a month.

The system is designed to protect spouses and children. This makes sense since when the program was created the average wage earner's life expectancy was 60 and therefore wasn't expected to make it till retirement.

Non-working and lower earning spouses can elect to receive benefits based on their spouse's earnings if this would result in a larger benefit. Spouses are eligible for 50 percent of the primary earner's benefit.

Divorced spouses are eligible for benefits based on their ex's earnings, if they were married for ten years, are at least 62 years old, and are not remarried.

Minor children will receive an income benefit until they are 18 should a parent who has paid into the system for forty quarters suffer an untimely death.

People considered disabled prior to age 22 can receive benefits based on a parent's record.

Those lucky enough to be born prior to 1954 can elect to restrict their claim to their spouse's record once they reach full retirement age. I call this the "get paid to wait" strategy as it allows them to grow their benefit to the max benefit at age 70. This often cuts the breakeven time to six years—76 instead of 82—and provides significant life insurance benefit for the loss of a spouses Social Security at death.

Don't rely on the helpful person at the Social Security Administration to assist in the decision. This is not their job. They are not trained to give advice!

That said, I know from experience with hundreds of clients that they do give advice—after all they are human and it's a human impulse to help. Take their advice at your financial peril. Widows and widowers are common victims of poor advice at a time of critical need. While not allowed to dispense advice, employees are required to explain the advantages and disadvantages of filing an application and the filing considerations so the claimant can make an informed filing decision. An Inspector General's investigation found that widows were claiming the wrong benefit 80 percent of the time![34]

My clients are often advised to take penny-smart but pound-foolish strategies—more now but less later. I've experienced cases of simply wrong information—people born prior to 1954 being told they can't claim on a spouse's record and let theirs grow. I've had a widow told by a Social Security Administration employee that she lost two years of her husband's benefit because he had not yet claimed when he passed away. Totally wrong. It added much stress in a time of devastation.

The reality is government employees do give advice. Bad advice. This is a financial code that you need to crack. Get it right by running your numbers. Get help if you need it.

TAXES AND SOCIAL SECURITY
WILL I PAY TAX ON MY SOCIAL SECURITY BENEFITS?
Yes, no, maybe.

Up to 85 percent of your Social Security benefit may be subject to tax depending on your "provisional income." This definition of income includes interest, dividends, wages,

---

34   "Higher Benefits for Dually Entitled Widow(er)s Had They Delayed Applying for Retirement Benefits," Office of the Inspector General, Social Security Administration, February 2018, accessed August 31, 2019, https://oig.ssa.gov/sites/default/files/audit/full/pdf/A-09-18-50559.pdf.

other pensions, and half of your Social Security payment, plus other imputed income imposed by local and federal laws.

If you are married and able to keep your provisional income under $32,000, you will pay no tax on your Social Security benefits. You will pay income tax on up to half of your benefits if your income is between $32,000 and $44,000. Over $44,000, 85 percent of your benefit will be added to your adjusted gross income and be taxed accordingly.

Your state may or may not tax Social Security as income.

If these numbers seem low, it's because they are. They were established in the 1980s with the intention of only affecting the rich. Congress did not index them for inflation, so now we are all "rich," or at least pay taxes on our Social Security as if we were.

STAY OUT OF THE PENALTY BOX

If you collect your Social Security benefit before your full retirement age, you will lose $1 in benefit for every $2 you earn in wages over $17,640 in 2019. This is a penalty in addition to the income tax. Be careful. If you expect to work in retirement, you need to account for this harsh penalty and now double count income and Social Security, as the latter may be reduced. At full retirement age, you can earn unlimited income penalty free. President Trump, for example, is surely collecting Social Security, and receiving family benefits for his minor child. You will, however, be subject to the income tax on your benefits outlined above.

This penalty may seem unfair, but there's a logic to it and a reward behind it. The logic is that policy makers are concerned that people who take a reduced benefit will suffer in old age. The government wants you to keep working!

THE GOVERNMENT PENSION CLAWBACK

WARNING: Some government employees who are eligible for pensions based on earnings on which they didn't pay Social Security tax will receive reduced Social Security benefits in most cases. If you work in such a job, you cannot trust your Social Security Statement! You will likely get far less.[35] Make an appointment at a local office and get a customized estimate. Since this is a print the computer-screen job, the information is likely to be accurate.

LEG TWO: EMPLOYER-SPONSORED PENSIONS
DEFINED-BENEFIT, CASH-BALANCE, AND DEFINED-CONTRIBUTION

Employer-sponsored pensions have traditionally been the second leg of retirement's three-legged stool. The style has

---

35   Social Security Administration. For details, see Government Pension Offset SSA Publication No. 05-10007 and Windfall Elimination Provision SSA Publication No. 05-10045.

evolved over the years. Today pensions take three prevalent forms.

The traditional pension is a defined-benefit pension. Defined-benefit pensions, with a few exceptions, are solely the responsibility of the employer. Employers contribute money to a pool that must pay out a defined-benefit, typically a monthly payment, to an employee once she retires. The monthly payments can range from a few hundred dollars to $18,750, depending on the plan. An employee's payments are based on salary level and the years of work for the company.

Only one in five Americans who work in the private sector have a defined-benefit pension, and the proportion has been dropping for years.[36] While the employer is responsible for making the investments and ensuring that they are managed for the sole benefit of the employees, employees must decide how to receive the benefit.

Here are some standard options.

- **Lump-Sum Payment:** Some pensions allow employees to take a lump-sum payment that can be rolled over into an IRA and managed by the employee. If this option

36 In 2003, 20 percent of private sector employees were covered by a defined-benefit pension, traditional or cash-balance, down from 35 percent in 1990, according to the Bureau of Labor Statistics. In 1985, 21.52 million Americans were covered. That number dropped to 17.22 million in 2003 according to the Employee Benefits Research Institute.

is elected, the employee becomes responsible for the prudent stewardship of the money.

- **Single Life Annuity:** This option converts the pension into a stream of monthly payments that will continue throughout the life of the employee. They will end, however, the month the employee dies.
- **Joint and 50 Percent Survivor:** This option provides a stream of payments based on two lives. The employee receives a monthly benefit while living. When the employee dies the spouse will receive half of her benefit until death, at which time payments cease.
- **Joint and 2/3 Survivor:** Same as joint and 50 percent except the initial payment is reduced and the survivor payment is two-thirds of this payment.
- **Joint and 100 Percent Survivor:** The initial payment is reduced but the income stream doesn't change upon death. It ceases, like the others, upon the survivor's death.
- **Single Life and Period Certain:** The pension is based on a single life but guaranteed for a period of years even if the employee dies. For example, if an employee elected a single life ten-year certain that paid $1,000 a month and died after receiving benefits for five years, the beneficiary would receive the $1,000 for five more years. After that, payments would cease.

This decision can be daunting. To make the perfect decision requires knowing when one and their spouse will die. That's impossible.

WHICH OPTION SHOULD YOU CHOSE?

Almost everyone would pick a generous survivor option save for the fact that it can mean a greatly reduced pension. More for a survivor always means less for the pensioner. Since the choice is irrevocable, it's important to consider many options and make an informed decision. Critical factors include:

- Your health and the longevity in your family
- Your spouse's health and longevity in their family
- Your overall financial situation
- Could your spouse live on 50 percent of your pension?
- What other sources of retirement income and assets that can be turned into income are available?

If a lump sum is an option, how do you feel about managing investments? How do you feel about leaving a legacy for children, grandchildren, or charity? A lump sum is better for this than an income stream. If you like to manage investments, this may be a good option.

Do you have permanent life insurance that could allow you to take the single life option, take more income while you are alive, and replace the pension should you pre-decease your spouse?

A key feature of most pensions is that they will not adjust for inflation. This means they will depreciate each and every year. The first check is the largest, in terms of spending power.

CASH-BALANCE PENSION

Cash-balance pension plans have become popular in corporate America. As life expectancy has increased, traditional defined-benefit pensions—which require companies to accumulate enough money to fund a stream of payments over an entire lifetime—have become a costly burden for many employers. Many have converted to cash-balance plans.

Like traditional pensions, the contributions and the investments are the responsibility of the employers. But unlike pensions, employees are shown an account balance to which they are entitled, not a stream of payments based on an earnings and tenure formula. Employers will typically contribute a set percent of an employee's salary to the investment pool, a characteristic that cash-balance plans share with defined-contribution plans. Once an employee is vested, typically five years, the employee can take the money if they leave the company. Upon retirement, an employee can convert the lump sum of money into annuity streams of income like defined-benefit plans. Alternatively, the employee can roll the money into an IRA and manage it for retirement. Another option is to take the money but not roll it into an IRA. (This option would expose the entire sum to income taxes.)

LEG THREE: DEFINED-CONTRIBUTION PLANS: 401(K), 403(B), AND 457 PLANS

Defined-contribution pensions shift the responsibility for retirement funding and investing from the employer to the employee.

Unlike traditional pensions that guarantee a benefit, defined contribution pensions guarantee a level of contribution, and even that is optional for the employer and subject to change at short notice. What is guaranteed, provided one's employer offers a plan, is the right for an employee to defer a portion of their income, tax free, up to a government set limit. Some companies, but not all, offer after-tax and Roth options. These allow employees to contribute after-tax dollars to the plan as well. In the case of the Roth option, both contributions and earnings can be withdrawn tax free at retirement provided the account was open for five years and the employee met age requirements.

The employee is responsible for making investment choices from those provided by the plan. Some plans do arrange for employees to secure advice for an additional fee.

The amount of money an employee ultimately has at retirement is determined by the amount of contributions and the investment gains, or losses, on those contributions. Annuity options typically are not provided, although employees could purchase private annuities upon retirement. Other options include leaving the money in the plan, rolling it over into an IRA, or taking the lump sum and paying taxes on the entire amount.

ALTERNATE LEGS
PERSONAL SAVINGS

Personal savings are an extension to the third leg of the retirement stool. Individuals can save and invest in a variety of instruments including bank accounts, mutual fund and brokerage accounts, Individual Retirement Accounts (IRAs), Roth IRAs, and variable and fixed annuities. Sadly, these sources are often neglected by people, as they are considered less tax favorable, more difficult to fund, and more complicated to manage than the convenient employer-sponsored plan. This is often a mistake.

Once you retire, these negatives become positives for many of these accounts. Your individual plans often have better tax treatment and more flexible and convenient options. One of the great ironies of retirement planning is that while working people love retirement accounts, when they retire they love individual accounts.

OTHER SOURCES OF INCOME IN RETIREMENT

The other sources of retirement income include:

- Working
- Inheritance
- Children or family
- Charity

Although each of these may be available at some point in retirement, they all have one thing in common: a person does not have much control over them. Even work—the component you can most control—cannot be counted on due to health and the vicissitudes of the economy.

HOW MUCH INCOME WILL YOU NEED? HOW MUCH CAN YOU COUNT ON?

These are the perennial questions, and rules of thumb have evolved to answer them. I'm sure, for example, that you've heard you need 70 percent of your income in retirement. Sometimes it's increased to 80 percent.

It's dangerous and foolish to rely on rules of thumb.

Your desired lifestyle will dictate your level of income needs.

How do you plan to spend your time?

- Travel?
- Move to less expensive or more expensive location?
- Golf every day?

- Enjoy free books from the library?
- Go back to college and pay tuition?

Your first step is to determine what your current life costs. The next step is to adjust those expenses for your expected or desired retirement experience.

Keep in mind that retirement flips many aspects of finance upside down. When you're working, for example, your financial life tends to be driven by income. That is, income drives taxes, spending, and savings.

In retirement, for most people it's expenses that drive income. Here's what I mean.

If I spend $5,000 a month and have $2,000 in Social Security, I must fill a gap of $3,000 from some source, assuming I'm not working, and the kids aren't kicking in. This expense determines how much income I need to realize, which itself determines the income taxes. If I spend less, then my taxes are lower. If I need more, then I must contribute more to society.

To put it another way, two households, each earning $100,000 during working years, will pay similar taxes, assuming similar retirement plan savings. In retirement, it will be their expenses, not fixed income, that typically drive their financial relationships to taxes and determine how large a nest egg they need.

When I teach my classes, I stress the need to project expenses accurately for retirement. It's not important to be exact, but it is important to be realistic. I had a client underestimate monthly expenses by $1,500—a fact I only discovered after they were retired for a year and constantly needed more money than expected from their accounts. This was no small matter. Given the 4 percent withdrawal recommendation, it takes $450,000 of assets to generate this much income. In this case, it changed a retirement that was flush with funds to one that must be carefully managed.

WHERE WILL YOUR MONEY COME FROM?

Now, as the CEO, you must put it all together, or hire a CFO to help. Again, expenses give you the target. You must then match up income sources. How many legs does your stool have and how much can you expect from each leg?

- Social Security estimates
- Defined-benefit pension estimate
- Cash-balance pension estimate
- Defined contribution plans
- Personal savings

Do not forget about your Uncle Sam. Your income sources will be mostly pre-tax, but expenses must be paid with after-tax dollars. For retirees, income taxes are extremely progressive, as the more money earned, the more income—

i.e., Social Security—gets taxed. Be sure to understand the tax laws of your state. Does your state tax retirement accounts and Social Security, for example, or give these income sources a pass?

My clients are often shocked and sometimes delighted when I show them how a move from the high-tax Northeast to the low-tax South, especially the no-income-tax Florida, can save thousands in income tax. A dollar not spent on taxes can be spent on lifestyle. A person who eliminates $5,000 in income tax and $5,000 in property taxes puts $10,000 back into their budget. At the conservative 4 percent withdrawal rate, this is the same as having $250,000 in an after-tax investment account!

Once you've realistically matched up your expected income and expenses, you will have a general idea of whether you are financially independent. Don't forget to keep a cushion for unexpected expenses. If you are short, you will need to figure a way to fill the gap with more income, more assets, or less expense.

SIMPLE STEPS TO MAKE IT BIG

- Document the legs supporting your retirement.
  - Secure an estimate of your Social Security benefit.
  - Determine your employer benefits. Estimate your pension if applicable.

- ○ Record the balances on your employer-sponsored and personal investment accounts.
- · Determine your current annual budget.

CHAPTER FOUR

ACCUMULATE THOSE ASSETS: WHERE TO INVEST?

Investment planning is often mistaken for retirement planning. This is akin to conflating your car's engine with all its other systems. Your investments are an important engine powering your retirement journey. They are necessary but certainly not sufficient for retirement success. Put in perspective, people face two important decisions when creating and managing an asset accumulation and income generation program for retirement:

1. Where to invest, or which container to use?
2. What to invest in, or what instruments, stocks, bonds, bank instruments, or commodities to put in the containers?

Let's tackle the first question first. What are the best containers for my long-term investing? Here I focus on two threshold issues: taxes and access.

BOXING OUT TAXES

Your investing options, for retirement and otherwise, are distinguished by two basic features:

1. How the investments are taxed at point of entry, growth, and spending.
2. What restrictions the government places on accessing the investments.

I categorize the accounts as:

- Tax Me as I Go, Bucket A
- Tax Me Later, Bucket B
- Tax Me Never Again, Bucket C
- Tax My Gains Later, Bucket D
- Tax Me Never, Bucket E

Let's focus on the characteristics of each.

BUCKET A: TAX ME AS I GO

These are often called after-tax investments. Professionals will also refer to them as "non-qualified" accounts. Income generated from investments in these accounts will be taxed as ordinary income in the year in which it's generated. Any dividends generated will be taxed as well. Growth is taxed as capital gains when the investment is sold and the gain realized. Capital gains and dividends are taxed at lower rates than income. My favorite rate is zero, which is the case if a person is in the 12 percent federal tax bracket or lower. Also, losses can be used to offset gains and even ordinary income in future years.

These accounts are typically bank savings, money market, CDs, mutual fund accounts, and stocks and bonds held in brokerage account. You face no access restrictions on using these accounts.

BUCKET B: TAX ME LATER

These accounts tend to be a person's favorite while working. The reason: Contributions are pre-tax—they lower your taxable income dollar for dollar. Growth is tax deferred. They produce fewer smiles in retirement, however, as each dollar withdrawn is taxed as ordinary income at the person's highest tax rate, even the growth attributable to capital gains.

These are our retirement accounts, the 401(k), 403(b), and 457 plans and traditional IRA.

They come with many restrictions, each designed to prod

us into doing the right thing. These include delaying gratification until retirement age and then taking at least enough to generate the taxes the government wants and needs.

A 10-percent penalty is imposed if money is accessed before age 59½, for example. Exceptions include disability, a first-time home purchase, qualified education expenses, birth and adoption expenses up to a limit, separation of service for 457 plans, separation of service and age 55 for 401(k) and 403(b) plans, and systematic withdrawals at age 55 for IRAs. Most recently, the penalty was removed temporarily as a response to the COVID-19 virus.

At age 72, mandatory minimum distributions commence. Account holders must start taking out income and paying taxes whether they want to or not. The amount is based on life expectancy and calculated by dividing your account balance on December 31 of the prior year by the IRS-given divisor. If one's spouse is ten or more years younger, then the IRS allows the use of a second, more liberal joint life expectancy table.

BUCKET C: TAX ME NEVER AGAIN

Like Bucket A, contributions to accounts in this bucket are post-tax. Like Bucket B, the growth is not taxed. And unlike either Bucket A or B, the gains, if accessed correctly, will not be taxed.

These are Roth IRAs and Roth 401(k)s, 529 plans, cash value life insurance, and municipal bonds.

These accounts come with far fewer restrictions than their pre-tax kin. Still, Roth IRAs have contribution levels tied to income limits. Also, if you withdraw gains before age 59½, there is a 10 percent penalty, plus income taxes will be due (with some important exceptions for first-time home purchases, medical expenses, and education expenses).

The big escape hatch for Roths is that contributions can be withdrawn tax- and penalty-free at any time for any reason at any age. These contributions come out first. So if a person contributed $5,000 a year from age 25 to 35 and the account grew to $100,000, she could withdraw $50,000 for whatever she wanted with no penalty and let the remaining $50,000 in gains grow for tax-free retirement income.

Section 529 plans are education savings vehicles. Their monies must be spent on qualified education expenses, otherwise penalties and taxes will apply.

The restrictions on cash value life insurance depend on the insurance company. If the policy is completely surrendered to access cash, ordinary income taxes will apply on the gains in the contract. Also, withdrawals may cause policy to lapse, at which point withdrawals greater than contributions will be subject to income tax. Life insurance must be carefully managed.

BUCKET D: TAX ME LATER, BUT ONLY ON THE GAINS

Like Buckets A and C, investments here are made with after-tax dollars. Like Buckets B and C, the growth of the investments occurs on a tax-deferred basis. When the money is withdrawn and spent, gains or growth will be taxed as ordinary income.

This tax characteristic applies to after-tax contributions to 401(k)s, non-deductible IRAs, and fixed- and variable-deferred annuities. They key is that there is no upfront tax break, but all growth is sheltered from tax until it's withdrawn.

There are many complicating restrictions. If money is accessed before age 59½, a 10-percent penalty will apply to gains on both annuities and IRAs. For annuities, gains come out first, the opposite of Roth IRAs. For IRAs, the non-taxable contribution is aggregated with pre-tax IRAs and funds are withdrawn on a pro-rata basis. There are no contribution limits on annuities. IRA contributions are limited to current IRS limits.

BUCKET E: TAX ME NEVER EVER

This is the triple tax-free bucket. Like Bucket B, contributions are made pre-tax. Even better, they avoid FICA taxation if made through payroll. Like Buckets B and C, the investments grow on a tax-deferred basis. Like Bucket C, the money comes out completely tax free if the rules are followed.

At present, the only legal option for such wonderful treatment is Health Savings Accounts (HSA).

As you can imagine, there are plenty of catches and restrictions to get no-taxation. To contribute to these accounts, one must have a qualifying high-deductible health plan with a minimum deductible of $1,350 for an individual or $2,700 for a family plan.

Contributions to the account are limited by the IRS. Limits in 2020 are $3,550 for an individual and $7,100 for those with a family plan. If you are 55 or over, you can add another $1,000. These funds can be invested in mutual funds and other securities. Withdrawals are tax free if used for qualifying health expenses per IRS publication 502. The list is quite expansive and includes Medicare Part B and supplemental premiums in retirement. Withdrawal does not have to occur in same year as the expense. Once on Medicare, people can no longer contribute to HSAs. They can still use the accounts—they just can't put any new money in.

STRATEGIC TAX PLANNING

To minimize taxes over a lifetime, it is important to think strategically about where you invest your money. As with most things financial, diversification is usually the wise choice.

Keep in mind that most of Social Security and defined-benefit pensions are Bucket B, making most of the monies taxable on the way out. Also remember that the tax people pay on their Social Security is driven by their overall income. Most people end up highly concentrated in Bucket B and therefore pay high taxes in retirement. I refer to this as the "tax time bomb."

Consider your family needs $50,000 of annual after-tax income in addition to Social Security and company defined-benefit pension to live in retirement. How much will you need to withdraw if all of your savings are in Bucket B and your average combined federal and state tax rate is 20 percent?

You will have to withdraw $62,500: $12,500 for taxes and $50,000 to spend.

If you are retired for twenty-five years, you will pay $312,500 in taxes.

If, however, you had invested in Bucket C, the "Tax Me

Never Again" bucket, you may be able to access half of that money without claiming it as income. This could lower your tax rate and mean you only need $25,000 of after-tax income from Bucket B, the "Tax Me Later" bucket.

Assuming a 15 percent combined tax rate, your family would only have to withdraw $29,412 a year: $4,412 for taxes and $25,000 to spend.

Total tax paid over your twenty-five-year retirement: $110,294.

This is a tax savings in retirement of 65 percent.

Personal finance conventional wisdom for years has insisted on maximizing contributions to employer-sponsored defined-contribution plans before funding other retirement alternatives. Today this is wrong for many Americans.

People who can expect modest incomes in retirement may find that taking too much income from the "Tax Me Later" bucket increases the taxes they pay on Social Security. At higher levels of wealth, that income will increase the premiums they pay for Medicare.

Social Security is tax free for married couples with taxable income up to $32,000. Up to half of the benefit is taxed at income range $32,000 to $44,000. Once a household income reaches $44,000, 85 percent of the benefits are taxed.

I once worked with a widow whose marginal tax rate was driven to more than 50 percent due to the taxes created by income generated by retirement plan withdrawals. One of the largest frustrations many of my middle-class clients have is the privilege of paying more for Medicare because they are forced to take income they don't need from their pre-tax retirement plans.

I am not against pre-tax plans. But you can get too much in them and wish you'd accumulated in a Roth or an unrestricted taxable account.

This has been backed up by academic research. A study by economists from the Federal Reserve Bank and Boston University found that a couple earning $50,000 a year fully contributing to 401(k) plan and earning 8 percent on the investments increased their lifetime taxes 6.4 percent and reduced their lifetime spending by 2.3 percent.[37]

The HSA is a surprising addition to the retirement account pantheon. It's not technically a retirement account. It's earmarked for healthcare. But most people will be forced to spend after-tax money on healthcare in retirement. Why

---

37 Jagadessh Gokhale and Laurence J. Kotlikoff, "Does Participating in a 401(k) Raise Your Lifetime Taxes?," May 2001, accessed December 23, 2004, http://econ.bu.edu/kotlikoff/401kfinal.pdf.

not spend never-taxed money? A recent study in the *Journal of Financial Planning* recommended that people max out their health savings accounts prior to investing in their employer plans.[38] After securing an employer match in the company 401(k), I often counsel clients to fully fund their HSA prior to moving to another account. The tax effects are that powerful.

THE POWER OF AN HSA

Want to accumulate a bucket of money that will never, ever, ever be taxed? Here's a strategy: sign up for a health savings account.

The health savings account is the Holy Grail of tax strategies. It avoids all federal income and payroll taxes when you contribute— an even better up-front tax-deal than an employer-sponsored 401(k) or personally maintained IRA. Like all tax-favored accounts, there are no federal taxes on the year-to-year income and gains in the account as it marinates. Here's the kicker: like a Roth IRA or 401(k), if the money is distributed for appropriate expenditures in a compliant way, there are no federal taxes when it's spent.

It's triple-tax free! No federal taxes, not even FICA and Medicare, so long as it's payroll deducted. Never. (States have the option

---

38 Greg Geisler, "Could a Health Savings Account Be Better Than an Employer-Matched 401(k)?" Journal of Financial Planning 29, no. 1 (2016): 40–48.

to tax contributions and gains. At present, three states tax contributions and two states tax earnings.)

There are plenty of catches, but none need to be too onerous. First, a person or family must have a qualifying healthcare plan. These plans have high deductibles—a minimum of $1,400 for an individual and $2,800 for a family in 2020. That's why the tax-free savings is blessed. Instead of sending the money to an insurance company tax-free to later have it potentially pay out for you tax free, you are paying yourself and retaining the money and the risk tax free. These are available in the individual market and increasingly at major corporations. One in four employers that offers health insurance includes an HSA eligible option.

Next the money needs to be spent on a qualifying healthcare item. The full list is available in IRS Publication 502. It's a fun read and you'll find that along with the predictable health expenses it includes such items as acupuncture, service dogs, and weight-loss programs. This is the same list used by the older and more familiar flexible spending account (FSA) that provides our frame of reference for the HSA. If you ever need the money for health-care spending, it'll be there for that traditional use. The big difference is that the FSA is a "use it or lose it" account—money unspent in each year is lost forever. The utility of the HSA is that the money can be invested and accumulate year over year.

This is where the mental shift and opportunity arises to build a substantial tax-free nest egg for retirement spending—even if it's not directly for healthcare. I often counsel my clients to put in as much as possible and never take a withdrawal from the HSA for a routine healthcare expense, such as a co-pay, that can be covered from regular income or taxable savings. (Again, if it's ever needed, it's accumulated for this purpose.) This leaves the money to compound tax-free for retirement. At that time, it can be used to cover the more than $260,000 per couple that Fidelity estimates they will need for healthcare spending.

But it gets even better. Under current rules, a distribution is tax free if it's used to cover a qualified healthcare expense. There is no requirement, however, that this expense and distribution occur in the same calendar year. The power play is to save healthcare receipts for all the non-reimbursed health spending and then, for whatever reason one wants, one can withdraw that much tax free at any time. Really. It's true. It can turn into a tax-free cruise fund.

Let's put some numbers on it. This example does not represent actual or future performance of any specific investment or product and should not be used to predict or project investment performance. Imagine a hypothetical 45-year-old who put in the max family contribution of $6,750 for twenty years and earned rate of return of 6 percent, compounded annually. At that rate—a hypothetical number that is certainly not guaranteed—she would have $248,302 after twenty years, when it's time for Medicare. She would have contributed $135,000. If she spent $2,600 annually out-of-pocket and saved the receipts, she'd have $52,000 that could be withdrawn at any time for any reason. If, however, she had spent the $2,600 from the account each year, she'd only have $151,556 at retirement. She'd also have to use all of it for future healthcare expenses. Not terrible, for sure, but depending on the person's financial status, it might not be as favorable as the first option.

Now this may seem too good to be true, but I assure you it's the current law of the land. The broad social-policy and economic trend is a shift from socialized benefits—either provided by government or corporations—to tax incentives for individuals and families to accumulate funds to protect themselves and prosper. Those who take the time to understand the rules will be the people who benefit the most. This opportunity, after all, lies at the intersection of three complicated areas: tax law, healthcare policy, and investments.

By far the biggest tax frustration I see in my practice is driven by too much pre-tax retirement money. The solution is to direct investment flows to taxable, Roth, and HSA accounts.

There is a limitation for investing in Roth IRAs. Taxpayers filing single lose the ability to contribute once their Adjusted Gross Income (AGI) exceeds $137,000. For married couples, the AGI limits are $193,000 for full contributions and fully phased out at $203,000.

For these people, the front door to the Roth is barred. There is a back door into the Roth IRA through which even the highest of earners can enter. It involves making a conversion of a traditional IRA, something anyone can do regardless of income. The catch is that income tax is due on the gains on the amount converted. But what if there are no gains? Then there's no tax! This is where the back-door Roth comes in. Non-deductible contributions are made to traditional IRAs and then converted. No deduction, no tax. The catch is that account aggregation rules apply, so it's only tax free if there are no other pre-tax IRAs. Employer plans don't count. This is an effective strategy for people to fund Roths each year.

TO ROTH OR NOT TO ROTH

If you are eligible for a Roth IRA and already participating in an employee plan, it may be advantageous from a tax and long-term capital accumulation perspective to contribute to a Roth IRA instead of a traditional IRA both for yourself and for a non-working spouse. Roth IRAs are also more flexible than traditional IRAs, as account holders retain access to their principal contributions at any time penalty free.

Life is full a trade-offs, and the true cost of anything is that which is given up to get it. In this case, the cost of a Roth IRA or 401(k) is the potential tax deduction that could have been obtained if the money went to a traditional IRA or pre-tax contribution to a 401(k) or employer plan. Given this framework, it's clearly advantageous to use Roth IRAs in years when you are in a low tax bracket. For pre-retirees this is often not the case until retirement. When I work with college graduates and other people starting in the workforce, I often ask, "Do you plan to earn more later than now?" The answer is almost always yes. When it is, I counsel Roth IRAs after the employer match is secured. This increases flexibility and lowers expected lifetime income taxes.

Back to pre-retirees. One other factor to consider is where you withdraw the money. For retirees planning to head to tax-friendly states, such as a person moving from high-income-tax Sacramento, California, to no-tax Reno, Nevada, it may make sense to contribute to a Bucket B vehicle, book the federal and state income tax savings, and then convert or withdraw in a more tax-friendly jurisdiction.

PLAYING THE TAX GAME

Anyone can now convert from a pre-tax account to a Roth IRA. This is an incredibly powerful tool that must be wielded carefully. Taxes will be owed on untaxed funds in the year of conversion, and there are no do-overs. Let's focus on some strategic uses:

· IRA conversions form the basis of the back-door Roth strategy. This requires earned income.

- Retirees faced with paying more for Medicare due to the Income Related Monthly Adjustment Amount (IRMAA) can reduce future distributions and the taxes they generate from pre-tax accounts by strategically converting funds to Roth IRAs. See Taxing Health, below. IRMAA affects people who earn more than $87,000. You will pay extra money for Medicare.
- Retirees with modest expenses looking to minimize income taxes, perhaps at the level of zero, may want to convert IRA assets to Roth IRA assets.
- Retirees interested in integrational wealth transfer with high-income adult children may want to convert at their lower tax bracket, so their children pull more out after tax when the asset transfers.

TAXING HEALTH

Blowing out sixty-five candles has traditionally been a liberating milestone for Americans. Not too long back it marked the traditional retirement age at which Social Security could be collected with no reduction and a job could be left behind without worries of qualifying for private healthcare. Our full retirement age has ticked up to 66 on its way to 67 for those born in 1960 and after. This shift is well known. The shock that's hitting newly minted seniors these days is that for some the escape from employer-sponsored health insurance to Medicare can feel like jumping from the frying pan into the fire.

Medicare is thought of as a good bargain. It's part pre-paid health coverage from years of working and part subsidized medical insurance. Yet for seniors whom the government considers to have high income—defined as having $85,000 or more income per person—Medicare starts to look like not such a great deal. The premium alone will triple from $134 a month to $428 a month, per person, for those with incomes over $214,000. That's just Part B. Throw in an average Part D premium of $48.50 in Connecticut, for example, and the $76.20 surcharge and the monthly tab jumps to $552. And this is for a program that only covers 85 percent of a person's expected healthcare costs. In addition to the expense of Part B and the drug surcharge, most people can expect to add the premium of a supplemental policy.

So what can be done?

Here are some strategies to stay out of the top 5 percent of income earners. The first line of defense if you're given notice of an increased penalty is to appeal. The system looks back two years to the most recent tax return. Has your situation changed for the worse, or better? Sometimes a person's income is increased by a deferred compensation plan or a monetization of unused sick days in the year of retirement. If this is the case, appeal to a local Social Security office to get the surcharge reduced. It never hurts to ask. The Social Security Administration has published five reasons that categorically allow the extra premium to be waived. These include "you or your spouse stopped working or reduced your work hours," a particularly useful one for new retirees.

Assuming you are stuck with the extra bill for at least one year, consider taking a big hit in one year to avoid smaller hits later. Call this the "tear the Band-Aid off" approach.

Consider a person who earns just $100 over an income threshold of $85,000 in 2017. This $100 in extra income will kick in $642 or additional Part B premiums and $159.60 of drug-plan surcharges. The marginal tax on this $100 of income is 800 percent! If this extra income is due to a required distribution from a retirement plan, this person could convert a portion of this IRA or employer plan to a Roth IRA. This would mean taxes paid today on the amount converted. But under current law, the Required Minimum Distributions (RMDs) would be avoided for future years and all earnings would be free of tax. For example, the first bracket ranges from $85,000 to $107,000 so the person could convert $21,900 of IRA into Roth IRA without further increasing Medicare premiums. Income tax would be owed on the funds, but they would not drive future income.

If the extra income is dividends, bond interest (tax-free interest from municipal bonds counts toward Medicare income), or capital gains distributions that are putting you into the taxation doghouse, evaluate what a transfer to a low-cost and flexible fixed or variable annuity would mean for your monthly budget. This can push current taxation to the future, at which time the rules, or your income, may be more favorable. Alternatively, in some cases a person may have an existing cash value life insurance policy that will accept and grow additional premium tax free.

Americans in their 40s, 50s, and 60s who are looking forward to retirement will want to look to Medicare as a cautionary tale of the government punishing success and rewarding those who save and invest in the government's tax-favored plans, which bring with them higher taxes later. The only defense against attacks on one kind of income is to have another. I call it the "whack a mole" defense. Like the carnival critter, we need a hole to pop out of that the government isn't currently beating.

PRIVATE PENSIONS AND ANNUITIES

Annuities and cash value life insurance can provide tax-deferred savings, death-benefit performance guarantees, and flexibility on when and how to access one's money.

ANNUITIES 101

Annuities can play important roles in a retirement asset accumulation and income plan.

Immediate annuities provide a guaranteed stream of income payments in exchange for a lump-sum purchase payment. These are not accumulation vehicles; they are income streams.

Deferred annuities offer the ability to save money for use later, either by turning it into an immediate annuity or withdrawing contributions and earnings.

Annuities have a unique ability to cause controversy in the personal finance community. Some advisors and many academics endorse them for the protection they can provide against both declines in financial markets and running out of income in old age.[39] Others attack them as too complex, too expensive, and too low return to be worth the trouble.[40] One reason for debate is that there are many kinds of annuities—just as there are many forms of personal transportation vehicles from Toyota Prius to Chevy Suburban—and each is designed with features to get a particular job accomplished. But just as a Prius fails at pulling a camper and a Suburban may be overkill for a childless urban couple, different annuities do different jobs.

Annuities can be categorized in four ways. They are either deferred or immediate. They are either variable or fixed.

---

39   Moshe A. Milevsky, PhD, "Annuity Fables: Some Observations from the Ivory Tower," *Journal of Financial Planning* 31, no. 12 (December 2018): 46-54.

40   Ken Fisher, "Ken Fisher: Why I Have Annuities," *Forbes*, December 1, 2014, accessed February 17, 2019, https://www.forbes.com/sites/kenfisher/2014/12/01/ken-fisher-why-i-hate-annuities/.

Annuities are generally long-term contracts designed to accept contributions; they allow these funds to potentially grow tax-deferred and eventually be distributed back to the contract owner.[41] They are not pensions but rather private contracts between individuals and insurance companies. They are designed to ensure that people receive both their principal and interest over a lifetime.

In my classes, I draw a timeline that starts with work; in the middle is retirement; and it ends, unfortunately and inevitably, with death. I ask my adult students to think of how a pension must work. During the period from starting work until retirement there needs to be an accumulation of assets. This is the deferred stage. Those assets must be invested in something. If that something is cash and conservative bonds, then the annuity would be fixed. This is because it will have a fixed rate of return at any given point in time. If a portion is invested in publicly traded equity securities, then it will be variable. This is because the value will fluctuate day by day, even minute by minute, with the value of the underlying securities.

While in the deferred stage, the annuity will not pay taxes on the gains. These will be paid when the money is withdrawn, at which time gains are taxed as ordinary income.

---

41 See Leila Martin, "How Do Annuities Work?," MassMutual, accessed May 8, 2020, https://www.massmutual.com/planning/articles/how-annuities-work.

At retirement, what happens to the lump of money? That is, if it's an annuity contract, how are the funds accessed?

One option is to transition the contract to its income phase. In exchange for the contract principal value, the insurance company will send out both principal and interest to the recipient each month in a steady check. In the private marketplace, these can be acquired with a lump sum of money without a deferral stage. This is called an immediate income annuity. Deferred annuities can also be annuitized at an appropriate time. Once on, the payments are typically fixed, although some companies offer variable payments and inflation-adjusted payments.

You will encounter annuities once called equity-indexed annuities that are now called fixed-indexed annuities. These are not some magic hybrid annuity. They are simply a version of a fixed annuity where the interest earned is determined by a derivative of the price movements on various equity indexes.

BANK, MUTUAL FUNDS, AND BROKERAGE ACCOUNTS

These taxable accounts can offer excellent sources of long-term accumulation of assets. If done correctly, they will help you manage taxes in retirement.

Bank accounts offer FDIC guarantees for balances under

$250,000 per person on the account and are typically most appropriate for a portion of savings that may need to be accessed on short notice. Accounts to use include high-interest money market accounts and certificates of deposit. Benefits include guarantees and liquidity, as well as access to money on shorter notice without risk of market volatility. Drawbacks include lower rates of return that may not keep up with inflation over time.

Non-qualified mutual funds allow a person to participate in securities market returns, be broadly diversified, and enjoy access to the money along the way. Benefits include diversification, access to money without government penalties, and lower capital gains tax rates for equity instruments. Drawbacks include paying taxes on any gains and income that are distributed each year.

Non-qualified brokerage accounts allow one to hold mutual funds, exchange-traded funds, individual stocks, individual bonds, and brokered CDs.

The advantages and disadvantages correspond to the bank accounts and non-qualified mutual funds, depending on the investment held. For individual stocks and exchange-traded funds, there is the advantage of controlling when capital gains taxes are triggered and being able to match gains and losses to minimize taxes. Dividends are taxed at preferable rates. In addition, there are estate-planning benefits to non-qualified accounts as the cost basis is stepped up upon transfer, resulting in zero capital gains taxes, and full market value can be deducted for charitable contributions.

Disadvantages of non-qualified accounts include paying taxes along the way. For individual securities, it's the difficulty of selecting good stocks and bonds. This can be mitigated by using exchange-traded funds or ETFs which, in their traditional form, are broad index funds that trade on the exchanges. These distribute few capital gains until owners sell them and allow investors the broadest diversification possible.

SIMPLICITY

With all of these choices, it can be a challenge to keep retirement planning simple. The key is to break the tasks and needs down and then match the right tool for each job, always being mindful of taxes. For example, we all need an emergency fund, often called a cash reserve. These funds—as the name "cash" indicates—should be set aside in a stable and liquid account. The first obvious choice is bank accounts, and certainly some if not all should be under the protection of the FDIC. Other options for potentially better returns include fixed annuities, and money markets and short-term treasury investments in brokerage accounts.

I will detail a powerful income-generating program later in the book, but to preview it here, consider breaking your assets into buckets with different time horizons. You may want three to five years of necessary withdrawals in an income reserve account or income reservoir. Each of the choices above is appropriate if properly layered for liquidity.

Next, for your intermediate and long-term investment money—and, yes, you have long-term money at retirement—you will most likely want a mix of mutual funds and exchange-traded funds (ETFs) that match your tolerance for volatility, otherwise referred to as "risk." You will want to locate them in non-qualified accounts, Roths, and pre-tax accounts based on your future income needs, tax projections, and, of course, where they already are. Most of us are heavy in pre-tax, and that's just how it is.

Finally, as part of an asset accumulation and income generation plan, you will want to examine the features and costs of annuities to determine if they will do a job that you need done. Farmers need tractors, but generally not Uber accounts. City dwellers may not even need a car. Such diversity exists in finance as well. A couple with Social Security and two corporate pensions already have four immediate annuities and may not require or want any additional income streams. A family with substantial spending needs and only Social Security may wish to devote a portion of their accumulated funds to purchasing an immediate annuity for another stream of income.

The bottom line is that personal financial planning is more art than science, and it needs to be highly customized to a family's needs and desires. Understanding your options and how they will be taxed and accessed is a necessary first step on this journey.

SIMPLE STEPS TO MAKE IT BIG

- Map out your retirement accounts by bucket.
- Determine if you have an HSA that you are not fully using.
- Pull out your most recent tax return, and determine your tax bracket.

CHAPTER FIVE

YOU'VE GOT YOUR CONTAINER—WHAT DO YOU PUT IN IT?

Investing is not the only component of retirement planning. It is, however, a critical component. If the investor gets it right, they will likely end retirement worth more than when they started. If a person gets it wrong, they will experience stress as they watch their principal dwindle.

Everything in life carries risk, and investing is no exception. Even if one takes no nominal risk with their money—they stuff $100 bills into a nuclear-war-proof safe in their basement—they are still subject to one of the most pernicious risks in retirement: the loss of purchasing power of money through inflation. Risks must be managed. They can never be eliminated. This must always be kept in the forefront of your mind.

Investing creates some risks and mitigates others. An investor must understand the specific risks he or she is taking with each investment and how these risks relate to other risks one faces in life and investing.

BASIC RISKS OF INVESTING: THE BIG THREE

The three big investment risks are business risk, systemic risk, and interest-rate risk.

- **Business Risk:** This is the risk that the company or government one invests in or loans money to goes out of business and cannot repay the money, or that the ownership position becomes worthless. Think of Enron, Lehman Brothers, and even General Motors, whose equity owners were wiped out even as the company survived due to government intervention.
- **Market or Systemic Risk:** This is the risk that external events, such as the mortgage-debt-driven financial crisis, 9/11, the oil shock in the 1970s, and most recently the Covid-19 viral pandemic, can cause a general decline in nearly all the securities in the market.
- **Interest-Rate Risk:** This is the risk that a dramatic change in interest rates will affect one's investments. An increase could lower the value of a bond portfolio,

for example, or decrease the value of stocks due to a more expensive business environment. An interest-rate decrease may lower the purchasing power for an investor who is relying on fixed-income investments to maintain a standard of living. This is the reality of the post-financial-crisis world from which we are only emerging a decade after 2008.

As you can see, any change can provide both opportunity and peril, depending on why and how one is investing. One risk may be an opportunity for another investment. Government bonds increased in value during the financial crisis. Later, as low interest rates punished people relying on bond instruments for yield, those people moved their money out of bonds and helped fuel rallies in dividend-paying equities such as utilities. The key is to know one's own risk, understand the risks of the investments one holds, and deploy one's resources in a smart and prudent manner.

OWNING VERSUS LOANING: TO STOCK, BOND, OR BALANCE?

Most financial instruments—when stripped of their fancy names and special packaging—are either a stock or a bond. That is, one either owns a stake in an underlying company or real property, or is loaning money to a corporation or a government.

Bonds, sometimes referred to as fixed-income investments,

are debt instruments. The fundamental transaction is that one provides money to a corporation or a government to use for a fixed time period. In exchange, the entity agrees to pay a set interest rate. Once the period has expired, say five, ten, or twenty years, the entity returns the person's money.

Debt instruments take on a variety of forms and names:

- Bonds
- Treasury bills
- Bank CDs
- Notes
- Debentures
- Fixed account
- Senior loans
- Bank loans

The advantage of debt instruments is that they tend to be more stable than equity investments. If one loans money to a stable company or a stable government, such as the US government, the chances of default are low and can be easily gauged. Debt investments are essential for shorter-term investments and for stable ballast to a long-term portfolio.

The disadvantage of bonds is that in general the value of the principal is eroded by inflation. Provide a government with $1,000 today, and it'll give you $1,000 back in twenty years.

The real value of that $1,000 in twenty years given even modest 3 percent inflation is a mere $549. Inflation cut the real principal value nearly in half.

Once issued, most bonds can be bought and sold in the secondary market. One can, for example, purchase a twenty-year-bond ten years after it was issued, collect the interest for five years, and sell it to someone else, who will ultimately receive the principal payment from the corporation.

Although a bond's interest rate is fixed, bond prices fluctuate daily on the open market. The prices of bonds will generally move in the opposite direction of interest rates.

This is why people can lose money in a "safe" bond. If they sell prior to maturity, the transaction absolutely can result in a principal loss, especially when the effect of taxes is included. Or it can go the other way; if interest rates fall, bond prices will rise.

Speaking of taxes, returns from bonds are taxed in two ways: the interest is treated as ordinary income; the gains are taxed as capital gains.

Consider this example:

Joe purchases a $1,000 ten-year bond issued by General

Electric with a coupon of 6 percent for $800 five years after it was issued. Joe likely gets his discount for one of two reasons. Either interest rates have risen since the bond was issued or GE's credit profile has declined. At any rate, he holds it to maturity, at which time GE sends him a check for $1,000.

Every year, Joe receives $60 in interest from GE. This is added to the first page of his tax return, and he pays ordinary income taxes on it.

When he receives the $1,000 from GM he will have earned a capital gain of $200. This will be taxed at the favorable capital gains rate—probably lower than income tax rates.

Bonds issued by states and municipal governments are free of federal tax. If they are issued in the state in which you live, they are generally free of state tax as well.

There are two types of tax-advantaged municipal bonds: general obligation bonds and revenue bonds.[42]

General obligation bonds are backed by the general taxpayers and the full faith and credit of the issuing government and its ability to generate the general tax revenue to pay

---

42 The federal government will not allow a tax exemption for municipal bonds that are issued to fund certain activities, such as for replenishing an underfunded pension and for essentially private projects even if nominally public owned, such as sports stadiums. Be sure that revenue bonds are exempt from federal taxation.

bondholder's interest. They are approved by the voters. They may support such things as schools or other capital projects.

Revenue bonds are issued by a municipality to support some project that is expected to generate revenue, such as toll roads or airports. Bondholders are repaid by the revenue from the specific project. No revenue, no payment.

Since municipal bonds are tax free, they can pay a lower interest rate per level of perceived risk than a corporate bond. To decide if a municipal bond is appropriate, calculate the effective tax-free yield of alternative debt investments that offer a similar level of risk.

Consider Doreen's choice. She has $100,000 she wants to use to purchase a lot in a lake community in five years when her children are old enough to be strong swimmers. She wants her money to work for her but does not want to take the risk that the stock market will be down when she needs the money. For her, bonds with a five-year maturity are a good option. She is in the 22 percent federal tax bracket. Her state taxes her at 5 percent. She is wondering if a municipal or taxable bond is a better choice, provided they have equivalent risk. A corporate bond will pay her 7 percent interest. A municipal bond will pay her 5 percent.

In which should she invest?

One can determine the taxable equivalent yield of a corporate bond by dividing the interest rate of the coupon by one minus the marginal tax rate. In general, the higher one's tax rate, the more attractive municipal bonds become.

Back to Doreen. She is paying a combined 27 percent in taxes on her last dollar earned. Therefore, a municipal bond paying 5 percent is equivalent to a corporate bond paying 6.85 percent. A corporate bond for her is a better deal, if it has an equivalent risk as the municipal bond.

Alternatively, if she was in the 37 percent federal tax bracket and 5 percent state, she should jump on the municipal bond, with its 8.6 percent equivalent yield.

ASSESSING THE RISK OF BONDS

There are two main risks of investing in bonds.

- Interest-Rate Risk: The longer the maturity, the more sensitive a bond's principal value will be to interest rates.
- Default Risk: This is sometimes referred to as credit quality. It is the fixed-income version of business risk. This is the risk that the issuing institution will not be around when it's time to pay back the principal.

There are three major sources of widely accepted information on the credit quality of bond issuers: Moody's, Standard & Poor's, and Fitch. They each use their own rating system, but each starts with Aaa or AAA and goes down from there. In the financial crisis, many bonds that were highly rated by these companies ended up being quite risky and defaulted.

Everything from lower medium and above is considered investment grade. This means that these instruments are compatible with an investment goal of preserving capital. Bonds with lower ratings are referred to as high-yield or junk bonds. Lower medium quality, which always has three B's, is the line between investment grade and junk. Because they carry increased risk of default, they generally offer higher yields or interest payments and the possibility for capital appreciation.

HISTORICAL RETURNS TO BOND INVESTORS

Bond returns are highly dependent on interest rates. In a period of high rates, the returns will be higher than in periods of low rates. That's the nominal return. The real return—return after taxes and inflation—is what matters for consumption and wealth preservation. In periods of low inflation, lower interest rates may still provide higher real returns than periods of high inflation and higher rates. For example, an 8 percent return can look great, but if you have 7 percent inflation, it's only netting 1 percent. A bond with a 4 percent yield in a world of 2 percent inflation actually performs better.

TAKING STOCK OF EQUITY INVESTING

Owning is the alternative to loaning and logically the means to a greater potential accumulation of wealth. This is because, by definition, wealth is the owning of assets. Equity instruments range from the familiar to the exotic:

- Real estate
- Common stock
- Preferred stock
- Commodities
- Real estate investment trusts
- Limited partnerships
- Collectibles

Purchasing stock is purchasing a portion of a company. Owners enjoy a right to share in its profits. They also partake in any loss in the company's value.

The advantage to owning versus loaning is that stocks historically have outpaced inflation. Invest in good companies and reap the rewards of those companies' growth. The flip side is true as well. If the company fails, an investor in common stock will typically lose their entire investment.

Dividends from publicly traded stock are distributions of the company's earnings and are taxed at favorable rates unless in a retirement plan.

When one sells the stock, any gain is taxed at a favorable rate, except if it's in a tax-qualified retirement plan.

WHAT'S THE BEST WAY TO OWN AND LOAN?

As always, the answer is that it depends on what one wants and needs. When it comes to retirement and income generation, the best solution is almost always a diverse blend. Let's examine how you are likely to hold and manage your investments.

MUTUAL FUNDS

Mutual funds are legal arrangements through which individuals can bundle together small amounts of money to form large pools of money and get professional-quality investing at a reasonable price. The money is managed by an investment company and is regulated under the Investment Company Act of 1940. The first mutual fund, still in existence today, is the Massachusetts Investors Trust. It was created in 1924. Today there are more than 9,300 mutual funds.[43]

---

43 Statista The Statistics Portal, accessed December 30, 2018, https://www.statista.com/topics/1441/mutual-funds/.

Mutual funds let ordinary people invest like multimillion-aires of a prior age. They can hire professional managers or caretakers or, if they prefer to index, buy a large number of securities to diversify risk, and have someone take care of all of the transactions and tax reporting. Mutual funds, indices especially, allow ordinary people to own every publicly traded company in the US economy for as little as $50 a month. For another $50 a month they can own the entire world economy. And for another $50 a month they can own a piece of nearly all the debt. This is quite remarkable and powerful.

TYPES OF MUTUAL FUNDS

Mutual funds come in many flavors.

Open-ended funds are the most common type of mutual funds that allow individuals to purchase and redeem shares daily directly from the company at the value of the investments the company holds at the end of the trading day.

Closed-end funds are a less common type of mutual fund that trades like a stock on exchanges. Once the individual securities are purchased, the manager doesn't change the mix of securities. The fund may trade below, at, or above the combined market values of the securities it holds.

Exchange-traded funds (ETFs), which are quite common

and increasing in popularity, are closed-end mutual funds that match various investment indexes, such as the S&P 500 or the Dow Jones Industrials.

Mutual funds are commonly classified by their investment objective. Here are some popular examples:

- **Money Market:** Funds that seek to keep the share price valued at $1 and offer short-term market rates of interest. They offer check-writing privileges.
- **Fixed Income or Bond:** Funds that invest primarily in debt securities issued by corporations, governments, government agencies, and government-sponsored corporations. Funds will specialize as government bond funds, corporate bond funds, foreign bond funds, or global bond funds. Within each specialization sub-specialties exist. For example, you can invest in a government bond fund that invests in Treasury Inflation Protected Securities or TIPS.
- **Growth:** Funds that invest in the stocks of companies that are expected to increase in value. Asset appreciation is favored over dividends.
- **Equity Income:** Funds that invest in stocks of companies that pay dividends. May invest in a limited number of bonds.
- **Foreign:** Funds that invest in non-US-based companies.
- **Global:** Funds that invest in non-US- and US-based companies.

- **Balanced:** Funds that invest in both stocks and bonds. Often, they seek to replicate a diversified portfolio.
- **Sector Funds:** Funds that invest in the stocks of companies in a single sector such as utilities, finance, healthcare, or natural resources.
- **Target Date:** Funds that invest in a range of investments designed to be prudent for a person retiring in a certain date range. These are popular in company-sponsored retirement plans and are often the default option.

MUTUAL FUNDS BY ASSET CLASS

Mutual funds are also often characterized by their asset classes based on a grid. For equities, there are two types of investing styles, value and growth, and three generally accepted market capitalizations: large, mid, and small. Large, for example, are companies valued at over $10 billion.

Management companies will use objective, style, and market capitalization categories to describe mutual funds. For example, large-cap growth, mid-cap value, or small-cap blend. Some funds may merely call themselves growth or value.

Always read a fund's prospectus to ascertain the exact securities in which the fund invests. Labels can be inaccurate.

EXPENSES

Mutual funds are tightly regulated, and as a result all the expenses associated with investing in them are disclosed to and quantified for investors every six months in prospectuses.

The expenses associated with mutual funds are management fees, sales charges, and marketing expenses. Each of these expenses simply reduces return and is already accounted for when mutual funds report their returns. The only exception to this is front-end sales charges. Let's examine the common charges.

Management fees compensate the management company for the tasks associated with security selection, purchase, and administrative overhead. In general, the larger the funds, the lower the management fees will be as a percent of holdings, since fixed costs can be spread over more dollars. More research means more expense, so large-cap stock funds are typically less expensive than small-cap funds, and domestic funds less than foreign funds. In addition, bond funds are less expensive than equity funds.

Here are the average asset weighted management fees:[44]

---

44 Patty Oey, Morningstar Services LLC, "Fund Fee Study: Investors Saved More Than $4 Billion in 2017. Our Study Finds the Largest One-Year Decline in Fund Fees," May 11, 2018, accessed February 17, 2019, https://www.morningstar.com/blog/2018/05/11/fund-fee-study.html.

US Equity	0.79 percent
Sector	0.88 percent
International Equity	0.71 percent
Taxable Bond	0.56 percent

Sales charges are also called loads: funds purchased directly from a mutual fund company typically do not have sales charges. Since the selection, purchase, and monitoring of the investment is done directly by the investor, there is no need to compensate an investment professional. Eighty-five percent of long-term mutual funds purchased are no load and are therefore either purchased directly or held in an account where the professional is paid by other means, such as a flat 1 percent fee.[45]

A minority of mutual funds purchased through a professional are often offered in two share classes, A and C.

- A shares contain a front-end sales charge. The maximum is 6 percent. There is no deferred sales charge.
- C shares do not have a front-end charge. They typically have a 1 percent deferred sales charge if sold within twelve or eighteen months of purchase.

Both no-load and load funds may contain a 12b-1 fee. This

45   2018 Investment Company Fact Book, A Review of Trends and Activities in the Investment Company Industry, 58th edition, Figure 6.11, accessed February 17, 2019, https://www.ici.org/pdf/2018_factbook.pdf.

fee operates like a management fee in that it is deducted from overall performance each year. It is designed for marketing and is commonly used by advisor-distributed funds to compensate the advisor for service and initial sales. It can be as high as 1 percent in load funds and no higher than 0.25 percent in no load funds.[46]

A successful investor will use a combination of these investments to mitigate risk and enhance returns. It's not difficult to understand why. What is more complicated is putting together the appropriate combination for one's unique financial plan.

Business risk, for example, is mitigated by using pooled investments that diversify even very small amounts of money over many companies. Mutual funds and exchange-traded funds allow anyone who desires the ability to protect themselves against the risk of any one company not executing on their business plan, failing, or committing fraud.

Allocating with pooled investments across multiple asset classes can, in some instances, insulate one from the systemic risks in particular market sectors. The dot-com collapse in early 2000s, for example, was most pronounced in growth and technology investments. Investors who were allocated to value and foreign stocks did not suffer loss in value of investments commensurate to growth and tech

46 Ibid.

investors. For true global crises, such as the 2008 collapse, asset allocation across equities did not provide the same salutary effects. Allocation to US government bonds did, however, provide safety.

Finally, interest-rate risk is addressed with diversification among fixed-income securities and asset allocation that does not over-rely on so-called safe assets for income. Interest-rate declines are perhaps the most damaging thing for retirees. In percentage terms they are far greater than changes in the prices of diversified baskets of equities and do far more damage to income plans of conservative people. It's a shame, but those things that are supposed to be the safest can be deadly if overdone. Even water will kill a person if she drinks too much of it.

SIMPLE STEPS TO MAKE IT BIG

- Examine your current investment statements to determine what proportion of your wealth is loaning and owning.
- Determine the investment vehicles you are using: individual securities, active or passive mutual funds, or exchange-traded funds.
- Examine your statements or use a web-based program or see a professional to determine the diversification of your underlying holdings and internal fees you are paying.

—

CHAPTER SIX

OPERATION ASSET ACCUMULATION AND INCOME GENERATION: PUTTING IT ALL TOGETHER

Money is better than poverty, if only for financial reasons.

—WOODY ALLEN

Now that you understand the tax consequences and restrictions of the buckets into which you can put your money and have a grasp of the different types of investments, stocks, bonds, annuities, and mutual funds, you must put it all together to form a cohesive portfolio. That portfolio must be designed to generate a lifetime of inflation-adjusted income.

We'll get to the actual portfolio in the next chapter. For now, let's focus on the system to manage the assets and generate and distribute the income. In my years of working with people, I've come to understand a critical fact: most people require three things from their finances in retirement.

First, you require safety of principal. You need to be able to write the largest check that you need to write, be it for an unexpected expense such as a home repair or a great vacation opportunity with the family.

Second, you need reliable income. By this I mean a similar, if not exact, amount deposited in a checking account on the same days each month.

Finally, and this is really the critical piece that is most easily misunderstood and neglected, you need this income to increase throughout retirement to keep up with inflation. Since, in my experience—and in retirement surveys—most people do not want to invade their investment principal and spend it down significantly, you also need a portion of this money to be invested for growth over time.[47]

The rub is that these three goals conflict with each other,

47   2018 Retirement Confidence Survey, Employee Benefits Research Institute and Greenwald & Associates, April 24, 2018, Figure 9, accessed February 17, 2019, https://www.ebri.org/docs/default-source/rcs/1_2018rcs_report_v5mgachecked.pdf?sfvrsn=e2e9302f_2.

at least insofar as they are implemented with financial instruments.

Consider your first need, liquidity, and safety of principal. Financial products that protect principal and provide liquidity—bank accounts and some fixed annuities and government bonds—do not grow and, as the last decade demonstrates, the income they generate is certainly not stable over long periods.

As for reliable income, most vehicles that provide reliable income—annuities, for example—do so at the expense of liquidity. In addition, they tend not to increase with inflation. Dividends from baskets of equity, for example, can provide inflation-adjusted reliable income, but these investments will certainly lose substantial principal value with some frequency. The prices certainly are not stable. They adjust every second on the exchange!

Finally, those investments that provide growth potential and potential for growth of income—a basket of common stocks and other equities such as real estate—do not in any way protect principal over any given period. You may be able to sell them, so they are marketable, but you will not want to sell them at a loss.

It's clear that no matter what you read, hear, or are pitched, there is no single solution, no silver bullet, to the task of generating retirement income. Everyone needs a system.

PRINCIPAL VERSUS INCOME

One of the great ironies of personal finance is this: Financial instruments that protect principal, by definition, let income fluctuate. Those things that allow principal to fluctuate tend to produce more stable income over time. People live on income, not principal, yet they focus on fluctuating principal, worried about temporary declines. In so doing, they often lock themselves into declining or downward fluctuating income.

BUILDING A SYSTEM

Let's move to the system. The first requirement is a goal. Life is like that. If you don't care where you are going, any road will do. That should not be the case for your financial plan.

Here's a goal: based on a detailed expense projection, a couple needs to generate $8,000 a month in pre-tax income. That's the need.

We then move to the resources this couple has available. Let's assume they have $4,500 in Social Security. Therefore, they need to generate $3,500 from investments. They do not have a pension.

The first issue to address is the size of the portfolio required to generate this income. This is another way of asking the question: how much income can safely be withdrawn from a portfolio?

The widely, although not universally accepted, answer to this question is 4 percent. This was developed by a financial planner William Bengen in 2004 and has been tested relentlessly since then with both real-world returns and academic laboratory modeling. The idea is that this is an initial withdrawal rate that can be increased for inflation over the years with a high probability of not depleting the portfolio. Pessimists on financial markets claim this may be too high.[48] Other researchers relying on historical data show that a rate could be higher if careful systems are followed.[49] For purposes of this example, we will use 4 percent. I consider it safe in my practice.

Using 4 percent, this couple would need a portfolio of $1,050,000. It takes a lot of assets to generate income, if one does not want to invade principal. Let's assume that they have $1,200,000 among retirement plans, bank cash, and non-qualified investments. If they didn't have enough,

---

48 For a book-length exploration of this view, see Wade Pfau, PhD, *How Much Can I Spend in Retirement? A Guide to Investment-Based Retirement Income Strategies* (McLean, VA: Retirement Researcher Media, 2017). For a shorter version, see Michael S. Finke, Wade D. Pfau, and David Blanchett, "The 4 Percent Rule Is Not Safe in a Low-Yield World," January 15, 2013, available at SSRN: https://ssrn.com/abstract=2201323 or http://dx.doi.org/10.2139/ssrn.2201323.

49 Bengen himself revised it up to 4.5 percent in 2006. For a good explanation of the more expansive view, see Michael Kitces, "The Ratcheting Safe Withdrawal Rate—A More Dominant Version of the 4% Rule," accessed February 17, 2019, https://www.kitces.com/blog/the-ratcheting-safe-withdrawal-rate-a-more-dominant-version-of-the-4-rule/.

they'd have to reevaluate their goals or go to a more aggressive withdrawal plan that would rely on using principal. Remember, most people do not want to invade principal. This probably applies to you. If not, you can have more initial income.

Safety needs to come first, and the first piece of safety here is to create an income reservoir. I often call this the operating account. This is a pool of money that will protect principal and be liquid when needed. Some people call this "unaffected assets," in that they are unaffected by stock market declines.[50]

As I noted earlier, I usually suggest three to five years of income. In this example, this creates a range of $126,000 to $210,000. This is $3,500 a month multiplied by twelve months by three and then five years. How these monies are invested will depend on options available in employer plans—many have attractive stable value funds that can't be replicated in IRAs—and the interest-rate environment. The key is that this is an expected income reserve, not emergency reserve, so each $42,000 needs to be available at the start of the year. Laddered CDs can therefore be used if the rates are attractive. For this example, let's put $160,000 or roughly four years of expected income into this account.

---

50 Jonathan Guyton, CFP®, "On Retiring into a Bear Market," *Journal of Financial Planning* 32, no. 2 (February 2019): 32–33.

This account is mandatory.

The next account to consider is what I call a retirement account. This is an annuity, typically a variable annuity with an income rider, although it could be a fixed-indexed annuity with an income rider. As discussed above, annuities are not very liquid; they have high fees that dampen returns or lower fixed rates if fees are low. So why use them?

Two reasons.

First, because they are expected over time to use both principal and returns to generate income, they can generate income at a rate greater than 4 percent, and in some instances, as high as 7 percent. This income will generally not inflate over time, but it will initially relieve pressure on the investment portfolio.

Second, they are hybrid accounts that combine two features that people find attractive and planners find useful: liquidity and guaranteed income. Unlike an immediate annuity that requires people to give up substantial sums to "purchase" a lifetime stream of income, these products allow people to retain access to the principal, subject to the terms of the contract. Typically, there are surrender charges that limit full access to investment values for a number of years.

It's important to be clear on the structure of the account. Money used to generate the income can't be removed in lump sums without affecting the amount of income. This is true of investment accounts as well, but it's more pronounced with annuities as the income guarantees are often greater than the account value.

For our example, let's move $200,000 into a variable annuity with a 6 percent income rider. This will generate $12,000 a year or $1,000 a month of income.

Since this income is initially guaranteed, it reduces our target need from non-guaranteed investments from $3,500 a month to $2,500, or $30,000 a year. Our income reservoir now covers more than five years of withdrawal needs.

The remaining $840,000 is invested in a total return investment portfolio consistent with the couple's tolerance for long-term volatility. I call this the Capital Account. If we assume a moderate risk tolerance, it will be between 60 to 70 percent equity. In years of positive market returns, this account will supply $30,000 a year of income. This is 3.6 percent of the account's value, which is in the safety range of the 4 percent rule.

Many years, this account will earn far more than its target, and this money can be redeployed into the reservoir for future safety or to replace past withdrawals, used for one-time purchases, such as once-in-a-lifetime vacations, or left in the account to compound. In flat and down years, withdrawals can be stopped and taken instead from the reservoir account.

This simple system is effective in generating reliable inflation-adjusted income. It is modular and customized for each person, depending on asset levels and tolerance for risk. More aggressive investors, for example, might forego the variable annuity.

People with surplus assets can elect to be more conservative or more aggressive, as they can absorb both financial market fluctuations and future inflation, two large risks, one short term and one long term.

People who have fewer assets may elect to use more annuity, as it employs the assets more aggressively, provides more income per dollar invested, and, for most products, provides a base of lifetime income.

Couples who do not care about legacy money—that is, money left over after they are gone—might elect more annuity for greater income early in retirement when they are both more likely to be around to use it and enjoy it.

This is a flexible, non-dogmatic approach to asset management and income generation in retirement.

MOUNTAINEERING AND THE SEQUENCE OF INVESTMENT RETURNS

One reason this system is so effective is that it addresses one of the largest risks a retiree faces—a down stock market early in retirement. This is merely dumb luck, but it can be devastating.

To frame the issue, ponder a popular question posed by retirement income planners. Imagine you're climbing Mt. Everest: what is your goal?

When I ask a large audience, most people blurt out, "Get to the top."

This is intuitive. Yet a few people, always after a pause, assert, "Get to the bottom."

This, of course, is the correct answer. It's to reach the peak and then make it down safely to tell the tale. I am told that descending the mountain is more dangerous than the climb.

Investing over the working years is the initial climb. The tools used are asset allocation, diversification, and dollar-cost averaging. The latter is the key means by which systematic investors accumulate more shares when prices are low, fewer when they are high, and therefore benefit from market volatility.

In retirement, this math reverses and becomes an enemy of wealth preservation. To generate the same income from total return portfolios, you sell different amounts of shares. When markets decline, the number of shares sold increases. If a decline happens early in retirement or often and deep enough, it can wipe out an investment portfolio and seriously impair a person's retirement.

This is the dreaded "sequence of returns" risk. The key is to avoid selling low. The income reservoir mitigates this risk by providing a pool of money, with a stable but low overall return, to provide withdrawals when the Capital Account takes a nosedive.

THEORY OF FINANCIAL DECLINES

The "sequence of returns" problem calls forth the important topic of market volatility—specifically drastic declines. In investments, the past is never a prediction of anything specific about the future. Past returns should never be relied upon for proof that any given investment is appropriate, good, or will perform well in the future. That said, financial markets themselves are broad complex systems that have years of well-studied and documented history. And just because specific downs and ups cannot be predicted with accuracy, you can take the fact that there will be ups and downs to the bank.

It's best to look at broad markets to know what to expect. Once you know what is normal, it can relieve some stress. It's like the two scariest rides at the California Disneyland when I was a kid: Space Mountain and the Matterhorn. These rides were scary because riders were in the dark and couldn't see the track. Understanding normal market fluctuations will show you the track. You may still lose your stomach from time to time, but you should get a system that will prevent you from losing your mind.

Looking at 117 years of the widely quoted Dow Jones Industrial Average, we can see how frequent declines are, with 5 percent pullbacks occurring, on average, three times a year, 10 percent pullbacks once a year, and 20 percent drops once every four years.[51] Yet over this period the Dow returned 7.32 percent without dividends reinvested.[52]

For the S&P 500, a broad index that contains the 500 largest publicly traded US companies, volatility is also the norm, not the exception. In an average, twelve-month span, it will decline 14 percent. These downs are the price paid for the ups. Over the last thirty-nine years, ending in 2018, it ended positive twenty-nine years, with an average return

---

51 "Keys to Prevailing through Stock Market Declines," American Funds 2018, accessed February 29, 2019, https://www.americanfunds.com/advisor/pdf/shareholder/mfgebr-051_recovrbr.pdf.

52 Kamal Khondkar, "Stock Market Yearly Historical Returns from 1921 to Present: Dow Jones Index," February 17, 2017, accessed February 17, 2019, https://tradingninvestment.com/stock-market-historical-returns/.

of 8.4 percent compounded.[53] This is without dividends reinvested.

Now few people only invest in large US equity position. Most also have bonds and other equity classes. But this is the most-quoted market and the one that defines most returns.

Given this reality, I often counsel people to think in units of four years. On a calendar-year basis, markets end the year up three years and down one.

THREE PLUS ONE EQUALS FOUR

If you retire at 65 and live to 95, you will have thirty years in retirement.

Divide 4 into 30 and you get 7.5. This means that on average there will be between seven and eight times in retirement when the US stock portion of your account is substantially negative on a calendar-year basis. It also means you will have twenty-two years that should be positive, again, based on historic relationships.

When the down year arrives, you face a choice. You can be

---

53 J.P. Morgan Guide to Markets, underlying data from FactSet, Standard & Poor's, and J.P. Morgan Asset Management, accessed February 17, 2019, https://am.jpmorgan.com/us/en/ asset-management/gim/adv/insights/guide-to-the-markets/viewer.

sad because your portfolio is down or happy because you only have five drops more to go! More importantly, if you can understand these relationships and believe in them, you can confidently build your income reservoir, switch your withdrawals to stable low-return assets, and avoid either downgrading lifestyle or depleting a portfolio. This is the key to a financially successful retirement.

SIMPLE STEPS TO MAKE IT BIG

- Determine your income needs from investments in retirement.
- Determine if you have enough investable assets to sustain this income on a 4 percent withdrawal. To do this, multiply the annual need by twenty-five.
- Create a reservoir of unaffected assets with three to five years of income needs.
- Consider the use of an annuity with income guarantees for a portion of these assets. Read the prospectus and consider fees and restrictions.
- Invest the remainder consistent with your risk tolerance.
- Consider your own theory of market decline and fluctuation.
- Get qualified professional help, if needed, for these critical steps.

CHAPTER SEVEN

THE FINANCIAL ENGINE THAT CAN

I am often asked, "What is the best investment for retirement?" A popular follow-on is always "Should I get more conservative—use more bonds—when I get to retirement?"

The answers are always the same.

"I don't know" and "It depends."

Creating a proper portfolio is more complex than simply subtracting one's age from one hundred and putting that percentage in stock and the percentage equal to your age in bonds.

It's important to be very goal-specific and begin with the end in mind by asking some questions. Specifically:

- **When do I need to access the money?** This defines your time horizon. People retiring in two years often think they have a short time horizon of two years. That's the horizon until they will need to take withdrawals. But their true horizon is until they don't need money any longer, which is death, usually very long-term. For some, it's effectively infinite, as they want to leave inheritance to children, grandchildren, or even great-grandchildren. I still have some of my great-grandfather's money. His time horizon for this money was certainly longer than his retirement age. So far, it's stretched to impact the lives of his great-great-grandchildren.

- **What is my current tax bracket? What is my expected future tax bracket? Higher? Lower?** These questions are important for asset location—Roth, pre-tax, and taxable, as discussed. The answers also influence the relative work of taxable and non-taxable bonds.

- **How do I feel about the risk of experiencing account-balance declines in down markets?** This is key, as the biggest mistake in investing is selling at the wrong time, out of fear. Being realistic about one's tolerance for downward volatility is important to avoid blowing it when crunch time arrives by turning temporary declines into permanent losses. It can be tough to see those negatives on account statements. Make sure you can handle it.

- **How do I feel about the risk of a reduced standard of living in retirement due to inflation?** Life presents a series of choices, small gambles in pursuit of larger goods. Life offers few guarantees or certainties. Some would rather reduce "sequence of returns" risk and market negativity by locking in low but stable returns. They increase the risk of loss of purchasing power due to inflation. Others would rather manage a flexible system that will likely drop in value substantially twice a decade but that promises increasing income and asset value over time. One of these views is not right and the other is not wrong. They do have consequences for investing and lifestyle. It's important to find your sweet spot.

- **Do I want to leave a legacy, or am I comfortable with spending down my principal?** The answer to this determines whether more conservative annuity-based income plans and portfolios are appropriate. If you are comfortable spending principal, these can manage many risks, but generally not inflation. For those who want to leave a legacy, using some income to purchase life insurance can be a good option. For people who do not want to invade principal, other strategies such as dividend investing will have to be employed. Depending on where you are in life, you may need to answer these questions for more than one goal: down payment for a purchase of a first house or vacation house, educating children, retirement, or taking care of dependent parents. For now, we'll focus on retirement income as the dominant goal.

MAKE YOUR PLAN

Once you have considered these questions, begin to put together a plan.

The first step is to assess your ability to withstand volatility or your risk tolerance. Two things determine this: how much time you have to reach your goal, and how you personally feel about and react to volatility.

You will then be able to produce a recommended asset allocation unique to your time horizon and your personal tolerance for risk.

For example, a suggested asset allocation for a 55-year-old moderate investor with the goal of retiring at 60 years might look like this.

Large-Cap Stock	35 percent
Mid-Cap Stock	5 percent
Small-Cap Stock	5 percent
International Stock	15 percent
Investment Grade Bonds	30 percent
High-Yield Bonds	5 percent
Real Estate	5 percent

This allocation of assets is designed to manage the risks to specific businesses and economic markets. It will not, as I discussed above, address systemic risk. That is, when recession hits or the entire financial market swoons, it will take the ride down. There will be times when all of the asset classes move together, both positively but more importantly negatively.

Standard categories for asset allocation include:

- Conservative
- Conservative to moderate
- Moderate
- Moderate to aggressive
- Aggressive

Asset allocation is an important factor that will determine your portfolio return for the long haul. Each planner and investment company will have unique mixes that fit these categories. This is the first clue that investing is as much art as science. The general consensus, however, is that each move up the risk-tolerance scale adds 20 percent equity or stock. So, for example, a conservative investor is 20 percent equity and a conservative to moderate will be up to 40 percent equity.

It's important not to isolate a single portfolio but to look at one's total assets when accessing overall risk. Consider my example from the previous chapter. With $210,000 in stable value investments, a person will be conservative to moderate in overall risk tolerance even if her Capital

Account is invested moderately. Each of your accounts should have a specific role, but one must consider the entire picture when accessing overall risk.

When investing, mentally apply the iron law of statistics. One rarely gets the average return on any given year, but you will get the volatility. Understand the volatility and what it means and be comfortable with it.

I cannot stress this enough. But in stressing it, I want to emphasize a counterintuitive truth.

You never need all your money at once!

Consider your asset and income plan. You are taking 4 percent of your money in a given year. If you have your income reservoir and your investments in the above moderate portfolio, you will be negative in a year of stock market decline. Your investments may go from $1,200,000 to $1,080,000 if the stock market suffers a normal decline.

You lost $120,000 or two and a half years' withdrawals. Not good. This is an accurate way to look at it.

Here's another accurate way: the intermediate bonds probably stayed flat at worst, at $400,000. The $200,000 of cash didn't decline at all. That provides over fourteen years of withdrawals at current rates—plenty of time for the stock portfolio to recover its value.

Now let's be a little more specific on some fundamental truths that will guide you well.

A dated but still widely cited study of pension fund performance found that just over 91 percent of the variation of portfolio performance can be attributed to the choice of the mix of stocks, bonds, and other asset classes. Less than 5 percent came from the actual stocks, bonds, and other assets chosen.[54] That is, the decision to have 60 percent of your portfolio in stocks is more critical to your long-term performance than the choice of what stocks, or stock mutual funds, to purchase.

Your allocation will dictate your long-run inflation-adjusted returns.

Once you pick it, stick with it and don't even think about outsmarting the market.

Studies show that it is folly for average investors to try to time the market by shifting in and out of asset classes based on speculation of what will be the next hot thing.

---

54   Gary P. Brinson, Brian D. Singer, and Gilbert L. Beebower, "Determinants of Portfolio Performance I&II," *Financial Analysts Journal* (July/August 1986 and May/June 1991).

The market moves quickly, and a few days, weeks, and months account for most of the return over a long period. Investors who try to time the market's moves pay dearly for guessing wrong. Over the last twenty years, if investors missed the market's ten best days, they missed out on 69 percent of its returns![55]

AVOID CHASING HOT TRENDS: A TWENTY-FIVE-YEAR STORY OF LOSS

1979: Hyperinflation, long gas lines, hostages in Iran. Experts advised against stocks. August 1979 cover of *Business Week*, "Death of Equities," and best-selling investment guru and author Howard Ruff's book, *How to Prosper During the Coming Bad Years*, said to steer clear of stocks in favor of hard assets such as gold, diamonds, and real estate.

What actually happened? From 1979 to 1989, an investment in stocks, as measured by the S&P Index, increased fourfold or 400 percent. An investment in gold lost value.[56]

---

55   Morningstar as presented in "Learning the Lessons of Time," Legg Mason Global Asset Management.

56   Dan Wheeler, "History Lessons," Investment Advisor, November 2004, Data from Bloomberg, L.P.

1989: That rising sun of Japan is poised to crush the bloated, tired, and worn-out United States, especially in manufacturing. This was the place to put your money.

What actually happened? From 1989 to 1999, an investment in the diversified S&P 500 index increased fourfold again, or 423 percent. An investment in the Nikkei Index, which tracks Japanese stocks, suffered a loss of 51 percent.[57]

2000: We are in a new economy and tech is king. Forget actual products and profits; the new economy is based on ideas and marketing. Forget asset allocation, at least if you listened to the Howard Ruffs of this decade, who advised to load up on new-economy tech stocks.

What happened? From 2000 through 2004, the tech-heavy NASDAQ lost 45 percent, having bottomed out at a 70 percent loss in 2003. The S&P 500, itself weighted heavy in some tech companies in the late 1990s, was down 18 percent. The broad US stock market returned an annual -1.4 percent; and bonds, as expressed in the Lehman Bond Index, returned an average annual return of 7.49 percent.

It's best to leave politics out of your investing as well. Studies show performance is politically neutral, at least with

---

57   Ibid.

respect to presidential party.[58] The S&P nearly tripled under President Obama, although he pursued more statist policies. Those who pulled out upon the election of Donald Trump missed a 24 percent increase in the first year.[59] It's not that policies don't matter—I'm sure they do. It's that the world is extremely complex, economies are linked, and there are thousands of factors that determine prices. It can't be predicted, managed, controlled, or gamed.

I don't know what the next hot asset class will be. You don't know what the next hot asset class will be. The investment guru who's making money selling books and newsletters doesn't know what the next hot asset class will be. Don't try to guess. Don't try to figure it out. Don't bet on it.

Success comes from time in the market, not market timing.

- Carefully develop an asset allocation consistent with your goals and personality.
- Select good investments in each of those asset classes.
- Rebalance your portfolio annually to maintain consistent allocation.
- Stay invested.

58 Sean D. Campbell and Canlin Li, "Alternative Estimates of the Presidential Premium," Finance and Economic Discussion Series Divisions of Research & Statistics and Monetary Affairs, Federal Reserve Board, Washington DC, 2004, accessed April 13, 2019, https://www.federalreserve.gov/pubs/feds/2004/200469/200469pap.pdf.

59 Returns Calculated on Political Calculations, accessed April 13, 2019, https://politicalcalculations.blogspot.com/2006/12/sp-500-at-your-fingertips.html#.XLHuLOhKiM9.

The secret of successful investing is that there is no secret. It's not a puzzle to be pieced together or an engineering challenge that can be precisely and confidently conquered for all time. At its core, it's a discipline that involves behavioral and emotional maturity and control. It's a mix of the logical, figuring out how much equity one should have to meet their goals, and emotional, developing strategies to process the inevitable and frequent declines in value without becoming too sad and stressed, as well as the even more frequent increases, without becoming too happy and irresponsible. Some people can achieve this on their own. Many people benefit from the assistance of a planning professional who can do much of the heavy lifting and provide support when it's needed the most.

SIMPLE STEPS TO MAKE IT BIG

- Consider the questions posed at the beginning of this chapter.
- Assess your tolerance for risk with a tool provided by a trusted financial advisor or one of your current investment providers. Use more than one if possible.
- Compare your current asset allocation to allocation suggested by your risk-tolerance analyses.
- Examine your feelings in the most recent declines in financial markets, and be very realistic about your ability to stay invested during significant declines in portfolio values.

- If you need or want assistance, seek help from a qualified professional advisor.

CHAPTER EIGHT

RISK MANAGEMENT

PROTECTING WHAT YOU
CAN'T AFFORD TO LOSE

We know only two things about the future: It cannot be known, and it will be different from what exists now and from what we now expect.

—PETER DRUCKER

Managing life's risk is the key to enjoying a life free of financial worry. Building assets is important; protecting the assets you've accumulated is critical. This is as true in retirement as it is on the road to it.

You cannot totally avoid life's risks. You can—and must—manage them.

We face two broad categories of financial risks.

The first category includes risks to property that would cause significant financial hardship—your house burning down, for example, or your car totaled in an accident.

The second category includes human risks—tragedies that affect people whom you either rely on financially or would have to support financially. These are life's real and unavoidable tragedies: the untimely death of a family breadwinner or homemaker, a person who is disabled and unable to work, a chronic medical condition that requires expensive treatment, or a parent or grandparent requiring expensive custodial care.

TYPES OF RISK

Risk can be addressed in four ways. Consider the risk of dying or being disabled in a motorcycle accident:

1. Avoid behaviors that cause it—don't ride a motorcycle.
2. Adjust to minimize consequences—wear a helmet, gloves, and leathers, and don't drive in poor weather.
3. Transfer risks to a third party—purchase life, disability, motorcycle, and liability insurance.
4. Retain risk—be prepared to accept consequences.

The options available will depend on the nature of the risk, its likelihood, and likely financial consequences. Which option, or combination of options, you select is a personal choice. It will, however, impact those who depend on you.

Risks can also be categorized by the likelihood of occurrences and the consequences if they come to pass. For example, a 30-year-old person is not likely to die. If this person is the breadwinner for a family, the consequence of his passing might have catastrophic consequences for those he loves. This category—not likely, but with severe consequences—is best suited for insurance solutions.

If a risk is likely—Evil Knievel becoming disabled—insurance will not be available at a good price, regardless of the consequences. These risks need to be minimized with safety gear and some portion of the risk retained.

Alternatively, a risk that is unlikely but of little consequence, such as a dorm-room refrigerator breaking down, should simply be retained.

We use insurance to prevent physical and human tragedies from becoming financial tragedies. The life cycle of risk typically transitions from protecting the capacity to earn income and therefore build assets to protecting the assets themselves.

A recent college graduate, for example, may start out with negative net worth due to student loans but valuable human capital, considering a combination of her emergent skills and long time horizon. She will spend the next forty years turning that human capital into income, a portion of which will be used to build up financial capital—investment accounts, vesting in Social Security, perhaps a pension. Over this time, she will pay down a mortgage and educate her children. It's easy to see that this woman, assuming she has children and a spouse, needs to insure her human capital with both life and disability income insurance. If she were a machine, not a person, this would be obvious.

As this woman approaches retirement, her needs may shift from primarily protecting her earning capacity to protecting the financial capital that it has amassed. That is, if she were disabled, she may be able to live off her accumulated monies. At this point, her insurance needs shift to storage insurance for her stored capital. The biggest risk to middle-class wealth is paying for long-term custodial healthcare, what I call paying rent in the wrong hotel. Once a person has accumulated assets, she or he needs a plan to protect them from this risk.

One risk that is not yet on the personal finance writers' radar screen, but I believe will emerge as the next crisis, is the lack of life insurance among retirees, especially in the early years. Consider a family that lives on $8,500 of monthly income, with $5,000 of it coming from Social Security. Assume this Social Security is a combination of two $2,500 benefits, a common fact pattern I see among two-income boomer couples. If either the husband or the wife passes away early in retirement—or at any time for that matter—the household will lose $30,000 a year in income. At a 4 percent withdrawal rate, that represents a loss of $750,000 of capital. Expenses may drop by $2,500 a month, but this should not be assumed.

The point: don't assume that life insurance is unnecessary once you retire. The main reason people purchase life insurance is to replace income. This reason may still exist for you at retirement, especially in the early years.

Here is another point to ponder. Just because a family can retain a risk, doesn't mean that it will choose to do so. Listening to a popular personal finance radio show a few years back, I was struck by how the frugal mentality can cost people a lot of money. A woman called about a neighbor's tree that had crushed her house in a storm. She said she was being told that it was her responsibility, not her neighbor's, as it was an act of God. This is true, and the host, who specializes in helping people cut costs in every area of their lives, said to contact her insurer and it will pay the bill. The caller, however, was out of luck. She paid off her house and cancelled her homeowner's insurance to save money. Big mistake.

That's why multimillionaires still purchase homeowner's insurance even though they could afford to rebuild their houses.

Another point: Risk must be transferred before it is imminent. I once read an article that counseled people to wait until they got sick to purchase long-term care insurance. I was shocked, as the writer and editors should have known this is not possible. In general, once insurance is needed, it cannot be purchased at a reasonable cost, if at all. Even the federal flood insurance program will not pay on a claim made within thirty days of purchase.

Finally, even good things, such as living a long life, create risk that ought to be addressed. Longevity increases the risks of running out of money due to excess withdrawals from a portfolio. This can be addressed with annuities. It also increases the risk of having the value of one's fixed-income sources be eroded by inflation, a risk that is exacerbated by most annuities. Again, a combination of approaches is required.

Let's examine some common assets and the financial tools that can address the risks common to them.

PROPERTY AND CASUALTY INSURANCE

Few people need convincing of the importance of home-owner and automobile insurance. These policies should be evaluated annually to ensure that they offer enough coverage. This is especially true for homeowner's insurance. As the cost of building materials and labor increases, you must be sure to have enough coverage to rebuild.

Here are some other important considerations:

Will your insurance pay for you to live somewhere else while your house is being repaired? For auto, will your policy cover the cost of a rental while your vehicle is being repaired?

Price is an important factor but should not be the only factor when purchasing home and auto insurance. Make sure the coverages quoted by different companies are comparable. Also, do you want to deal with a company directly, or would you prefer a local agent on whom to rely?

It pays to retain risk. Small claims are expensive for companies to administer and will eventually increase a policy holder's premiums. Therefore, it's often wise to retain as much risk as possible. You retain risk through a deductible.

DON'T FORGET YOUR UMBRELLA!

An umbrella liability policy picks up where your home and auto insurance leave off should you be involved in an accident or incident that winds up in a lawsuit. For example, a $1 million umbrella would cover you up to $1 million should you be sued. This will extend your $300,000 auto and home liability by $700,000. (You must have all your policies with the same carrier.)

HEALTHCARE

Surprise! Retirees spend more on healthcare in retirement than before. This is one expense that is likely to increase over time. According to the Bureau of Labor Statistics, households headed by people age 25 to 34 spent just over $250 a month out-of-pocket on healthcare in 2017. This jumped to more than $500 a month on average by age 65.[60] (Fifteen years earlier, these respective figures were less than half, at $120 and $250 a month.[61])

There is a wide variation on the estimates of what retirees will spend on healthcare. A widely cited study by Fidelity asserts that the average couple will spend $285,000 over a retirement.[62] This a laboratory projection, however, and includes all the premiums paid to Medicare. A longitudinal study of actual retirees from 1990 until now finds that Americans spend a lot less out-of-pocket—$27,000 per person.[63] This is in addition to Medicare premiums.

HEALTH SAVINGS ACCOUNTS

For those who have time to plan, health savings accounts—

---

60   Bureau of Labor Statistics Survey of Consumer Expenditures 2017, Table 1300, Age of Reference Person, accessed April 13, 2019, https://www.bls.gov/cex/2017/combined/age.pdf.

61   Bureau of Labor Statistics Survey of Consumer Finances 2002.

62   "How to Plan for Rising Health Care Costs," Fidelity, April 1, 2019, accessed April 13, 2019, https://www.fidelity.com/viewpoints/personal-finance/plan-for-rising-health-care-costs.

63   Sudipto Banerjee, "Cumulative Out-of-Pocket Health Care Expenses after the Age of 70," Employee Benefit Research Institute, April 3, 2018.

that "Bucket E" asset described in an earlier chapter—may be an attractive option for early retirees. They combine a high-deductible catastrophic insurance policy with a double-ended tax-free IRA.

- Insurance kicks in after you pay a minimum deductible of $1,350 for an individual or $2,700 for a family.
- Individuals can contribute an amount up to $3,550 to a savings account in 2020. The limit is double for families. The contribution is tax deductible. The money earns interest or grows in mutual funds tax free. If it's spent on healthcare, it is not taxed on the way out. If a person is over 55, they can contribute another $1,000. That is the limit for both individual and family plans.
- The maximum 2020 out-of-pocket, including deductibles and co-payments but excluding premiums, is $6,900 for an individual and $13,800 for a family.

These plans can be a great relative value for many Americans, as they allow people to pay lower premiums, invest the savings in a tax-free account, and accumulate it for the future when the money will be needed. Details are always important, and these plans must be compared to others available in the marketplace and matched to the unique health needs of the purchaser. The investment features are great, but they should be secondary considerations to your overall healthcare needs.

THE ABCD'S OF MEDICARE

Medicare is the national health insurance program for senior citizens.

Part A is mandatory, funded by payroll taxes, and covers hospital use. It's not comprehensive, and seniors need to be aware of its limitations.[64] Here are some key details as of 2020:

- It has a per-benefit period deductible, $1,408.
- If you are in a hospital more than sixty days, you must pay $352 a day in co-insurance.
- For hospital stays 90 to 150 days, the coinsurance is $704 a day.
- Over 150 days, it pays nothing.
- It doesn't pay for care needed while traveling out of the country.
- It doesn't pay for blood.
- It doesn't cover out-patient prescription drugs.

Medicare Part B is often referred to as physician insurance. It is optional but highly subsidized by the general taxpayer. Its monthly premium is deducted from your Social Security check. It is $144.60 a month in 2020. (As discussed

---

64 "Medigap: Covering the Gaps in Medicare," NOLO Law Center, www.nolo.com, accessed December 30, 2004. For up-to-date coverage and cost, see "Medicare Costs at a Glance," Medicare, accessed April 13, 2019, https://www.medicare.gov/your-medicare-costs/medicare-costs-at-a-glance.

earlier, this premium increases once a person earns more than $87,000.) It too has limitations, including:

- The annual deductible is $198.
- There is a co-insurance payment of 20 percent.
- It doesn't cover dental care.
- It doesn't cover eyeglasses, hearing aids, or eye exams.

Medicare Part C, or Medicare Advantage (formerly Medicare+Choice), allows seniors to choose an HMO, PPO, or HSA company to provide the combined benefits of Part A and Part B. Plans can offer more comprehensive benefits, and most do. They can charge for them, and many do. The benefit of Part C is that it eliminates the need for Medigap Coverage (see below). Medicare Advantage programs are not available everywhere and are more prevalent in densely populated areas.

Medicare Part D is the drug benefit plan. It's complicated and far from comprehensive, and it is voluntary.

- Seniors with incomes greater than $12,123 must pay a monthly premium that on average is $32.50.[65]
- They will pay a maximum deductible of $435. Part D

---

[65] "Medicare Part D Premiums Continue to Decline in 2019," Centers for Medicare & Medicaid Studies, July 31, 2018, accessed April 13, 2019, https://www.cms.gov/newsroom/press-releases/medicare-part-d-premiums-continue-decline-2019.

will then cover 75 percent of drug costs between the deductible and $6,350.

- With total spending over $6,350, Medicare will cover 95 percent.
- In addition, a $2 co-pay applies for generic drugs and $5 co-pay applies for brand-name drugs. If you're in a nursing home, co-pays are waived.

Your total out-of-pocket, before the government picks up 95 percent, is more than $7,000 annually.

Medigap insurance is a highly regulated supplement that covers the gaps in Part A and Part B programs. One can enroll at regulated premiums without any evidence of insurability in the first six months after signing up for Part B. The ten plans, A–J, are standardized, but the premiums will vary by carrier.

All in, here is what an average person might pay for Medicare monthly. Remember, it's an individual program. Married couples will pay double.

Medicare B	$135.50
Medicare D	$32.50
Medigap	$155.00
Total	$323.00

DISABILITY INSURANCE

As people approach retirement, they are often in peak earning years, minimal expense years, and investing a significant portion of their income. A question to ask:

Who would pay your bills and fund your retirement if you couldn't go to work tomorrow?

This risk of being disabled is much greater than the risk of death for working Americans.

This risk can be transferred through disability insurance. Disability insurance pays a weekly or monthly income benefit after a person has been disabled for a predetermined amount of time called the elimination period. It pays for a predetermined period of time: six months on the low end up until 70 years old on the higher end. There are even plans today that will make contributions to simulated retirement plans, allowing you to keep your retirement on track.

People acquire disability income insurance in a variety of ways. For many, the first stop is group insurance. Many employers offer group long-term disability insurance for employees. Common features include the following:

- It pays after 90 or 180 days.
- It replaces 40–60 percent of base salary. It doesn't

include bonuses or pension contributions. It is often capped at $5,000 a month.

- If the employer pays the premium, the benefit is taxable.
- The benefit won't increase with inflation.
- It integrates with Social Security. (For example, if your company plan pays $3,000 a month and you are determined eligible for Social Security's disability benefit of $1,500 a month, your group plan will reduce its payment to $1,500 so that your total is still $3,000.)
- It's not portable between jobs.

Group insurance can provide great base protection. It is not a full-income replacement plan, however, and I've had clients become shocked and angry when they were put on Social Security only to see their group plan's income reduced dollar for dollar.

This brings us to private disability insurance. You can purchase a private disability income contract either to stand alone, if you don't have a group plan, or to supplement a group plan. Common features include the following:

- Elimination periods are one month to two years.
- Benefit periods are six months until you are in your seventies.
- Benefits are tax free if you pay the premium from personal funds.
- Benefits can increase with inflation.

- Premiums can be locked in never to increase. Policy can never be cancelled by the insurer.
- Premiums vary depending on occupational duties. Welders will pay more than attorneys.
- Benefits are not affected by Social Security.
- The policy is fully portable between jobs and even if you change occupations.

Many pre-retirees will grow out of the need for disability income insurance. But most people will require this important coverage for most of their working years. I encourage clients to use a mental trick. Think of yourself and your spouse not as people, but as money machines. Ask, if you have a machine in your basement printing $60,000 a year, how much would you insure it for? Most people say as much as possible.

LONG-TERM CARE INSURANCE

Paying for long-term custodial healthcare is the most devastating risk to middle-class wealth. Like retirement income planning, no silver bullet exists to satisfactorily address this issue. In my planning practice we use a suite of tools including asset ownership, family, and trusts. Long-term care insurance is an important tool in the toolbox. Long-term care insurance, either as a standalone plan or as a rider on a life insurance or annuity contract, provides tax-free money to pay for a person's custodial care should they have trouble performing two of five basic activities of daily living or if they suffer from a brain disease such as Alzheimer's.

The Five Activities of Daily Living:

- Toileting
- Bathing
- Dressing
- Eating
- Transferring

An American's largest risk in retirement is outliving his or her money. For most Americans, if they are forced to pay for the custodial care of a spouse or themselves, they have a good chance of running out of money.

The average annual cost of nursing-home care in the United States is $89,297 a year for a semi-private room and $100,375 for a private room.[66] It's much higher in many places. Here are some costs of semi-private rooms:

New York, NY	$145,088
Washington, DC	$109,500
San Francisco, CA	$109,777

---

66 Genworth Cost of Care Survey 2018, accessed April 13, 2019, https://www.genworth.com/aging-and-you/finances/cost-of-care.html.

The average cost of home healthcare workers is $22 an hour nationally. Again, it's more expensive in many areas.[67]

Do you have an extra $100,000 in your annual retirement budget to pay for a second residence or house staff? If not, you need to consider transferring a portion of this risk.

WHAT WILL MEDICARE PAY FOR?

Medicare is health insurance and pays for skilled care, not custodial care. It will pay for some care, provided restrictions are met:

- It will pay for skilled in-patient rehabilitative care provided that patient was in a hospital for at least three nights and transferred to the facility within thirty days.
- The patient must be making progress toward recovery.
- It will pay for only one hundred days.

WHAT WON'T MEDICARE PAY FOR?

- Non-rehabilitative home care
- Adult day care
- Assisted living
- Skilled nursing facility over one hundred days

---

67 Ibid.

WHAT WILL MEDICAID PAY FOR?

Unlike Medicare, Medicaid will pay for institutional custodial care. The problem is that Medicaid is a welfare program for poor people. For Medicaid to pay, a person, and her spouse, must be considered poor.

WHAT WON'T MEDICAID PAY FOR?

- Home care in many cases
- Adult day care in most cases
- Assisted living in most cases

Medicaid is a joint federal state program and specifics vary by state, but in all cases people must be financially needy to qualify. In Connecticut, here is how to qualify for Medicaid.

For a married couple, the stay-at-home spouse can keep no more than $126,420 in investments, bank accounts, and retirement plans. The institutional spouse's income—pension and Social Security—goes to the nursing home. The non-institutional spouse can keep her income. If it's less than $3,161 a month, she can use some of her spouse's income to top it off to a level determined by the state government.

If a person is single, they must spend down all their financial assets to $1,600. This includes cash-value life insurance, IRAs, annuities, investment properties, and brokerage accounts. A lien will be placed on the house. A person can keep a prepaid funeral contract, term life insurance, personal property, and the $1,600.

DON'T PAY THE WRONG HOTEL

If Americans make it to retirement with a nest egg, the primary risk that will deplete it is paying rent in the wrong kind of hotel—that is, the need for long-term custodial care. Prices for such services vary greatly by region. The area in which the majority of my clients reside, the Northeast, claims the highest costs in the country. I see each month how sending $10,000 to $12,000 from a portfolio to a nursing home or home care provider decimates a lifetime of wealth accumulation.

Insurance can be an important piece of the plan to fund these costs. But as prices for care have increased and interest rates have remained low, insurance companies have quit issuing new policies, raised prices drastically on the policies they will still issue, and increased premiums on existing, in-force policies, after securing permission from state regulators. All but the wealthiest Americans clearly need a multifaceted strategy.

If any area in financial planning requires the assistance of intellectually qualified, practically trained, and appropriately licensed professionals, it's long-term care planning. Writing large checks from accounts requires no skill or knowledge, but arranging one's assets, investments, and expenses so as to provide a loved one with needed care while not impoverishing a spouse is devilishly tricky. The strategies involve applying laws and regulations from the federal, state, and sometimes local level. What is allowed in some states can't be done in others. It can even vary by county in the same state. Find a professional in your area to assist in designing a plan. If you need it, time will be of the essence.

Each of us has a default long-term care financing plan. It's simple. We spend all our money, and then the state government, through a federal partnership known as Medicaid, picks up the tab. For some, Medicaid will be the inevitable backstop after a modest nest egg is depleted. For others, Medicaid may in fact be the goal after a period of self-pay and substantial assets are "protected." Most of the strategies involve some shifting of assets from a person who'd have to spend them down to a person or trust owner who is exempt. The general rule is that state governments will examine a family's financial records closely looking for non-market transactions within five years. If such transactions are discovered, the family will be required to pay the money back.

Residential real estate is a substantial asset in middle-class America. While you are married, the value of a house is protected so long as one spouse is residing in it. For a single person, the government will put a lien against the house value to recover the cost of care. There are multiple strategies to protect and utilize a house.

A house can be protected simply by not owning it. Houses can be transferred to relatives or trusts and, so long as the transfer took place five years prior to needing care, the asset will not be at risk. Provisions can be included on deeds or trust documents that provide a person the right to live in the house for as long as they live. This is often called a life use.

Other ways to protect the value of a house include having a child live with a parent to keep them from needing services for a period of time. Again, this is all state dependent. A person with a disabled child, even if an adult, can exempt the value of the house. Another unique strategy involves selling a house and using the proceeds to purchase a life use in a child's house. This protects the purchase value, as it was a market transaction, not a gift.

This is a key distinction. Gifts in a five-year period trigger disqualification. Market transactions, provided they are really market transactions, can be okay. Other examples of market transactions that can shift from available assets to exempt assets, or from a person who must pay to those who don't, include the following:

- Purchasing a more expensive house for a spouse. Spending on needed maintenance, such as a new roof, driveway, heater, or air-conditioner.
- Purchasing a new car for a spouse. A car is an exempt asset.
- Creating market value contracts to pay children or relatives or friends for services they are providing. Examples are home care services or even financial management.

These are just general ideas that I have seen employed to meet family goals. The key is to develop a plan that fits your family's finances, goals, and values. Develop it with a knowledgeable professional well in advance of needing it. And hope, that like many disaster plans, it's never activated.

LIFE INSURANCE—PROTECTING INCOME

If someone you love depends on you or your income, chances are you need it. In a nutshell, one purchases life insurance because they love someone, owe someone, or both. Life insurance is a "contract" with an owner, an insured, and a beneficiary. If the insured dies, the insurance company pays the face amount, tax free, to the beneficiary.

People need life insurance for different reasons at different stages of their lives.

In the early-accumulation stage, when mortgages are large, children need to be educated, and retirement plans are in the building stage, life insurance funds these unfunded liabilities should something happen to a bread winner. It allows a family to accomplish its goals.

In the late-accumulation stage, mortgages are often getting paid down or gone, children are launched, and a couple is in the home stretch of aggressive retirement savings. Life insurance protects the retirement savings for the surviving spouse.

Once retired, a couple enters the protection and distribution stage. A family may be depending on a pension for income. They certainly will be reliant on Social Security and assets saved over a lifetime. Life insurance can be necessary or useful to protect a pension payment should the recipient die, make up for reduced Social Security payment should a spouse die, and protect a spouse against fluctuations in an IRA portfolio or depletion of investments for paying for long-term care services. Other uses include providing funds for the lifetime of care for an adult child with special needs, and transferring assets, tax free, to the next generation.

How much life insurance does one need?

This is an area of much misunderstanding and a place where it's important to ignore rules of thumb such as two times-, ten times, or twenty times salary. Everyone's needs are unique. It's best to do your own personal math.

There are two basic methods of calculating a need. The first is referred to as the human life value. This straight-forward method simply figures what a person would earn until retirement, subtracts out taxes and what the person would consume, and then figures out how much money that would be in current dollars.

The second approach is often called a basic needs analysis. This method examines the actual expenses that would be involved if one died, the things a family would want to take care of, such as education for the children, paying off mortgages and other debts, and income replacement. It then calculates a figure based on these basic needs.

If a family is living on 100 percent of their income, which is often the case, these two approaches will produce similar results. One difference is that expected future salary increases can be built into a human life calculation. Families must be careful not to underestimate the amount of future income a young earner would produce.

The value of one's services must be protected as well. When a primary earner dies, income needs to be replaced but expenses will generally go down. When a homemaker dies, expenses will increase.

Here are some questions to ask yourself if faced with a loss of a spouse.

- Will I be able to keep my current job, or will I need to make a career change to a less demanding and less lucrative profession?
- Who will take care of the children while I'm at work? Day care? A live-in nanny? Family?
- How long will my children need constant care?

For retirees, a lot of these liabilities will be gone. The focus is on replacing income that will be lost, such as Social Security and pension. Wealth replacement is also an issue. If a long-term care need strikes, assets earmarked for income may have to be expended. A prudent life insurance program can replace this wealth when a person passes away.

WHAT KIND OF INSURANCE?

Insurance comes with many features and many names, but there are two fundamental types: temporary and permanent.

Temporary Insurance

Temporary insurance is called term insurance. These contracts cover a person for a set number of years: one, ten, fifteen, twenty, and thirty. It can have adjustable premiums or level premiums over a period and then adjust. It is pure insurance, like auto and home. If you don't get unlucky and use it, there is no residual value.

Over the last few decades, it has consistently gotten better and cheaper. If you are healthy, you can now purchase term that does not expire until you are in your eighties.

As with anything, term life has advantages and disadvantages. The primary advantage is price. Young healthy people can purchase big blocks of insurance for low premiums. It allows young families to cover temporary needs with temporary insurance. Insurance is always an expense and the premiums make it clear and understandable.

The primary disadvantage is that premiums increase over time, which makes it unaffordable for older people. Each contract term has a level premium, but one will likely outlive this contract and then face higher prices. This means that very few policies pay a death benefit, roughly 1 percent. If a family has permanent needs, this will not provide the protection it needs.

Permanent Insurance

Permanent insurance is designed to last a person's lifetime and ultimately pay a death benefit. It combines term insurance with an investment account in which premiums grow on a tax-free basis. These cash values are owned by the contract owner and can be accessed for use while the person is alive for such things as college funding, cash reserve, and retirement funding. Some policies allow the cash to be accessed as a withdrawal of premium. Others require the cash to be loaned.

Permanent policies differ based on how the cash value is invested, who controls the investment, whether the premiums are flexible or fixed, and whether the death benefit is flexible or fixed.

Whole life is the name for traditional permanent life insurance. The cash values are invested by the insurance company in its general account, which is comprised mostly of fixed-income investments. Premiums are fixed, as is the death benefit. Participating policies will pay dividends that can be used to offset premiums or purchase additional insurance.

Universal life policies are similar to whole life in that the cash value of this policy is invested conservatively by the insurance company. It differs from whole life in that it never pays dividends. Its premiums are flexible as is its death benefit. Modern contracts can offer lifetime guarantees for death benefit regardless of cash value.

Variable universal life is a contract in which the cash value is invested by the contract owner in variable subaccounts that provide access to professional money managers. These are generally equity, fixed income, and a guaranteed interest account. Premiums are flexible as is the death benefit. Some modern contracts offer guarantees for death benefit that are not dependent on cash values.

Many people will obtain life insurance through their employer. This employer-sponsored life insurance, with a few exceptions, is typically group term. The advantages are that it's easy to get in open enrollment and reduced underwriting, especially within thirty days of being hired.

If a person is very young or in poor health, the premiums can be less expensive.

It arrives with some significant disadvantages. An employer usually does not offer enough face amount to cover a person's need. The term insurance is usually not portable at low prices. Changing jobs means changing insurance or losing insurance. It can be significantly more expensive than private contracts for people in good health.

You must be very careful if you are relying on group life. You are not the client; the company is. I had a disabled client with a short life expectancy. He was on disability and getting a benefit until normal retirement age, 65. After a year, however, he got a COBRA notice, which meant his company was terminating him. With this termination he lost $500,000 of group life. I had another person at this same company get a termination notice five weeks prior to death. His family lost $90,000.

Survivorship Life

Survivorship policies, often called "joint life" or "second to die" policies, are single contracts that cover two lives and pay a single benefit upon the second death. They are permanent contracts and can be whole life, universal life, or variable universal life. They are commonly used in estate planning and for capital transfer. They can be good ways to ensure a trust is funded for a child with special needs.

There is no "best" life insurance contract or type. The type that best fits a family's needs will depend on many factors.

Risk transfer or insurance plays a critical role in an advanced market economy. At its core, it allows for people and organizations to take risk and flourish. In this way, it is absolutely a positive piece in the puzzle of economic activity.

In terms of individual financial planning, however, it should always be thought of as a necessary expense. There are some risks in life that simply can't be invested for; they must be insured against. Planners like me, who have the privilege of working with hundreds of families, know the randomness of both positive and negative surprises. I've had clients win lotteries and work for companies whose stock made them wealthy. I've had 35-year-old parents of infants who contract cancer. I've had more than one client die prior to finishing the plan. I have many others in their eighties going into their nineties. We must protect that which we can least afford to lose.

Rational people often attempt to be amateur actuaries: calculating if the premium of a disability or long-term care policy, for example, is worth it. There is no way to know. It's a negative lottery ticket. If it's needed, a person could never have invested for the return necessary to generate the money created. If it's not required, it's just an expense. As a consumer, you need to ask not about the probability of the negative event occurring, but rather about the consequence for you and the people who you love if it does. The premium must fit into a budget and not cause the problem it's designed to prevent, poverty. But in many cases, it's akin to a utility bill, a necessary expense that indirectly enhances life and secures and protects prosperity.

SIMPLE STEPS TO MAKE IT BIG

- Consider the range of risks that could derail your retirement plans.
- Gather and analyze your current protection portfolio of insurance policies to ensure your risks are covered at a reasonable cost. Utilize a professional if needed.
- When it comes time to sign up for Medicare, treat it like planning for a substantial vacation. It's a new system to you. After a few years, it will seem easy.

CHAPTER NINE

PLANNING YOUR FINAL ESTATE

TRANSFERRING YOUR ASSETS TO WHOM YOU WANT IN A TAX-EFFICIENT MANNER

If you want to see what your family and friends think of you, die broke, and see who comes to your funeral.

—GREGORY NUNN

Everyone needs an estate plan.

There are two aspects to an effective estate plan:

- Ensuring that your assets are managed well while you're alive if you are unable to do so yourself.
- Ensuring the tax- and fee-efficient transfer of your assets to whom you want, not to whom the government selects once you have left this world.

Estate planning can be as simple as having updated wills, durable powers of attorneys, healthcare directives, and the proper beneficiaries named on one's retirement accounts and life insurance.

When there's substantial wealth involved, it can be more complicated. It can also get more complicated if one has a dependent with special needs or if asset protection is an important goal. In these cases, trusts, strategic gifting, charitable activities, and smart use of life insurance can minimize taxes and maximize the amount of your assets that go to people and causes that you support, rather than state governments.

BASIC DOCUMENTS WE ALL NEED
LAST WILL AND TESTAMENT

Your will is the basic document in which you determine how your estate will be distributed and to whom. You will want to consider:

- Who will take care of any minor children
- Who will get what percentage of your assets
- Who will receive any collectibles or special items
- Who will be the executor of your estate

Don't die without a will. The government then will decide who gets what, including the care of your children.

Every financial plan I complete tells clients to get a will if you don't have one or make sure that it reflects your wishes if you do have one. I recently lost a client who had a stroke less than a year after retiring. Last time I saw her in my office, I said, "You need to marry your twenty-five-year life partner." I recommended a will many times. I got the call from her partner after she died. All the beneficiary forms were in place, and the corporate pension had a certain period payment on it that protected the partner. The problem: her house, owned solely by her, was to go to her father, who happened to be spending down assets, suffering from dementia, and would likely hit a nursing home.

Get a will!

DURABLE POWER OF ATTORNEY

This document allows someone to make decisions on your behalf and take care of your finances should you become unable to do so for yourself. It can be a general power of attorney, allowing a person to do pretty much anything you could do, or a limited power of attorney, which limits them to, say, paying the light bill.

If you don't have a durable power of attorney and become incapacitated, a court will appoint a person. Your affairs can be contested and will become public. Don't let this happen. Get a durable power executed and in place.

You will need a healthcare directive. This is a durable power of attorney that grants someone the power to make healthcare decisions for you should you be unable to do so for yourself.

You will want to execute a living will. This documents your intentions regarding end-of-life issues.

ASSET TRANSFER

As indicated, a will is extremely important. That said, many assets will transfer by another means. The options for transfer are:

- Will and probate
- Direct transfer accounts
- Joint ownership
- Trusts

PROBATE

The probate process is a court-overseen transfer of assets. It is orderly and well defined. All the estate's assets are delineated. All claims against those assets are settled, and then the remainder of the assets is distributed per the instructions of the will, if it exists, or through the state intestacy law, if no will exists.

However, it is a public process. Do you want your neighbors

to know how much you are worth and who you are giving your property to? And it can be expensive, as lawyers and executors and court fees will be paid from the estate. It can take a long time, well over a year to get things settled. That said, it is a formal process that offers judicial oversight.

DIRECT TRANSFER ACCOUNTS

- IRA
- Life insurance
- Annuities
- Brokerage and bank accounts with direct transfer designations

While the asset value of these accounts will be included in your taxable estate in most cases, the actual assets will transfer directly to the named beneficiaries upon your death.

Be sure that your beneficiaries are up to date. The designation on the account is final. It trumps your will.

The advantages of direct transfer include the swift transfer of assets outside of the probate process and the ease and low cost to altering your plans. The use of beneficiary forms and transfer-on-death forms can radically reduce the amount of your estate being subject to the probate process.

JOINTLY TITLED ASSETS

Joint Tenants with Rights of Survivorship (JTWROS): This is common for bank and brokerage accounts for married couples. All of the assets should be available immediately for use by the surviving owner.

Tenants in Common: This form of ownership grants each owner half of the assets. Upon death, the half belonging to the deceased would be distributed through his estate. The other half continues to be owned outright.

Community Property: In community property states—Arizona, California, Idaho, Louisiana, Nevada, New Mexico, Texas, Washington, and Wisconsin—both husband and wife own half of marital assets. Upon death, they transfer similarly to JTWROS.

Benefits of jointly titled assets include swift transfer and ease and continuity of management. For larger estates, jointly titling assets can limit estate planning flexibility. This is especially true for unmarried domestic partners. If my client's house, for example, had been owned jointly, it would have remained with her partner.

TRUSTS

Trusts can be used to own, manage, and transfer assets.

Every trust has a grantor, the person who places the assets in the trust; a trustee, the person or organization that manages the assets; and a beneficiary, the person or persons for whose benefit the trust exists.

There are two basic types of trusts: intervivos, or living trusts, and testamentary, or trusts created in a will.

In addition, a trust can be either irrevocable, which means the grantor gives up all rights to control the assets, or revocable, in which case the grantor can retain access to the assets. The former are typically used to minimize taxes and protect assets, while the latter are used to manage assets while living and transfer assets outside of probate.

Advantages to trusts for asset management and transfer include the following:

- Trusts are private. If assets are owned by a living trust, they will pass outside of probate according to the trust document. The transfer will not be public record and will be harder to challenge.
- Trusts can minimize expense, especially if property is owned in more than one state.

Disadvantages to trusts for asset management and transfer include the following:

- There is expense to creating and maintaining trusts. Assets must be retitled with the trust as the owner.
- One must find a competent trustee.
- A will is still needed to tie things together.

DEATH AND TAXES

Will your death be a taxable event? For 99 percent of us, the answer is no.

Federal law allows each person to transfer a set value of assets to anyone they choose free of tax. Any assets over that set amount are subject to an estate tax, payable by the estate. The tax is due nine months after the person's death. The estate is valued on the day of the person's death. In addition, a husband and wife can transfer an unlimited amount of assets to each other. Taxes will be due on the second death.

Most people no longer face federal estate taxes thanks to recent legislation that raised the amount an individual could pass tax free to $11,580,000. It's double for couples. Nineteen states have estate or inheritance taxes, some as low as $1 million.[68] So it still may be an issue at the state level.

---

68 Kay Bell, "Estate Tax: How It Works and Which States Have One," Nerdwallet.com, October 12, 2018, https://www.nerdwallet.com/blog/taxes/which-states-have-estate-inheritance-taxes/.

The way to reduce estate taxes has always been to minimize one's estate. The strategies used include strategic gifting, trusts, and charitable giving.

- Each person can gift $15,000 a year to anyone they choose, as many people as they choose, without any tax implications.
- Qualified education expenses do not count as a gift for tax purposes. For example, Grandpa Tom could pay Harvard tuition for grandchildren Jane, Jennie, and John at $70,000 apiece and still gift them $15,000 each in the same year.
- Charitable contributions are fully tax deductible in the year in which the IRS deems the contributions given, subject to limits as a percentage of taxable income.

These three factors provide the ingredients to the tax reduction stew cooked up by financial planners and estate-planning attorneys.

These days, with death taxes in abeyance, the focus of much advanced estate planning for middle-class Americans is asset protection. The threats: the nursing home and heirs paying income taxes on your yet-untaxed assets. The latter is called income with respect to decedent or IRD for short.

I've outlined the risk of long-term care in prior sections. The estate-planning tools to address this risk involve transfer of individually and jointly owned assets—not IRAs and employer plans—to irrevocable trusts. Houses and brokerage accounts can be protected with advanced planning. Income may even be acquired from the trusts, and the house can be lived in until death, but the actual ownership of the assets will have transferred from an individual or couple to a trust. In this case, if enough time has elapsed from transfer, the assets will be protected from Medicaid spend down.

Finally, estate taxes are not the only funds due to the government at death. IRAs, the investment gains in annuity contracts, and the untaxed value in employer plans will all be subject to income taxes when the funds are withdrawn. Strategies to address this include Roth conversions and life insurance to replace the income tax owed. For most people, this will be an issue for the next generation. Still, if splitting assets equally among children or other beneficiaries, a person should always consider the taxes due on certain assets to determine and adjust inheritances.

SPECIAL PLANS FOR SPECIAL PEOPLE

Sometimes it's necessary to do upside-down financial planning. I say this because the goal for most households is building and protecting assets to generate income to support financial independence. But for the millions of households with a member with special needs, wealth may be the enemy. Near poverty may in fact be the goal.

Depending on the need, a person may be eligible for and require large amounts of government assistance for daily living, housing, employment, and social activities. Eligibility for this assistance traditionally runs through a state's department of social services and requires a beneficiary to be financially destitute. Without adjustment, it's a classic Catch-22. A person needs the supports to live, but such supports are usually not enough to support a person in the lifestyle a parent wants for their child. Yet if that person has enough funds to supplement the assistance, the assistance is withdrawn.

Fortunately, governments and attorneys have created work-arounds for this dilemma. It is critical to work with a knowledgeable attorney who is familiar with the laws and administrative bureaucracy in your state. As a father of a special-needs daughter, I know this. What follows is a brief outline of basic strategies.

The first rule is, with the exception of an ABLE account, your family member should have very little money in her name. Funds should be held in special trusts called "special needs" or "supplemental needs" trusts. The purpose is to "supplement" but not supplant the support provided by publicly funded social service agencies. These trusts are set up by a third party and can be funded in a variety of ways, including cash contributions, inherited assets, and life insurance. They key is that the assets are directly deposited in the trust and therefore never become the asset of the individual with special needs.

It's critical for people with special family members to communicate with other family members about their financial planning. Otherwise a generous gesture, such as an inheritance directly into the child's name, can wreak havoc and ultimately go to the government to pay back services that were otherwise zero cost to the beneficiary. The solution is to make the trust the beneficiary. Problem solved. The trust itself can have a beneficiary so that when the family member passes, its contents carry on the legacy.

DON'T DROP THE BALL

IRA expert Ed Slott, CPA, asks a great question, the answer to which hammers home the importance of accurate and ongoing estate planning. A football team is up twenty-eight to three going into the halftime locker room. Has it done a good job?

The intuitive answer is yes. Ed accepts it, and then corrects, exclaiming, "We don't know yet!" The team is off to a good start, but it's only the score at the end of the game that counts. Don't blow it in the fourth quarter.

It's easy to blow it. You will be remembered for it.

Ponder the fate of the dropped ball. "Mickey Owen Dies at 89; Allowed Fateful Passed Ball," headlines the *New York Times* when the man who made the phrase "dropped the ball" meaningful.[69] Owens was a catcher for the Brooklyn Dodgers who dropped a third strike that cost his team a win. It was one of the few errors he made that year, a year in which he won an award for defense. Yet, it was an error, not the success, that earned him a place in history.

It's easy to drop the estate-planning ball. Having old beneficiary designations sends the retirement plans to an ex-spouse rather than children. Not updating beneficiary forms sends money to the most recent spouse, rather than the children who are on the forms. Absence of durable power of attorney with gifting power means investments are systematically liquidated and the house is sold to pay back your state for Medicaid assistance for custodial healthcare. Lack of a will means a parent, already on state aid, inherits your house. It becomes one more thing that is liquidated.

Don't let any of this happen to you or your loved ones. You've taken the time to accumulate wealth and implement and manage a plan to sustain it even as you turned it into a lifetime of income. Don't fail to plan for its preservation

---

69   Richard Goldstein, "Mickey Owen Dies at 89; Allowed Fateful Passed Ball," *New York Times*, July 15, 2005.

and successful transfer to the people and institutions that are important to you. It all starts with a simple plan.

SIMPLE STEPS TO MAKE IT BIG

- Review your current estate plan to confirm it accomplishes your wishes. Make sure you have an up-to-date durable power of attorney and healthcare directive.
- Review each of your beneficiary designations to ensure your money will transfer to your desired recipients.
- Consider the use of trusts to accomplish more advanced goals or asset protection, privacy, or protecting beneficiaries.
- Seek qualified professional assistance to draft and implement legal documents.

CHAPTER TEN

———

WRAPPING IT UP

We began at the beginning, and now we've come to the end. This project started more than a decade ago, designed as a workbook to accompany eight hours of group presentation. I took my title from a quote I heard attributed to Grateful Dead front man Jerry Garcia. Although it all seems simple enough to me, more than one non-industry reader informed me that I'd either have to change the title or change the text. I liked the title so elected to simplify the text as much as possible and insert simple steps you could take at the end of each chapter. I accepted that there was no way to provide simple answers for such a vast topic as personal financial planning. The details can be a bit daunting, but they are important. What's right for one person is wrong for another, and the only way to know this is to understand the range of possibilities. This is true for every area of financial planning, from the right goals for the right person, to the amount of money they must amass for financial security, to the investments they use, the tax strategies they employ, and the legal structures they use to protect and ultimately pass on their remaining wealth. I wanted to provide you with an appreciation for the range of options and simplify them enough so that you could make smart financial choices.

I'll leave you with a metaphor of life's financial plan as a journey. In the old days, when planning a significant road trip, a logical starting place was the AAA Office, where one could literally get a Trip Ticket. This included road maps, hotels, fueling stations, and even the traveler's checks to safely pay the bills without worry about highwaymen. You could make a journey like this as precise as you wanted, calculating the gallons of gas used, prices paid, hotels nights purchased, and even food eaten. There were some vagaries, of course, as a gas-price spike could increase fuel costs and summer road construction could delay travel times. But these trips could be turned into an engineering problem with plenty of certainty. I know, I crossed the country twice by car by age 27.

Personal financial planning requires a similar approach, but with far less certainty. First, you have to decide on your destination, or do you? Sometimes it's about the destination and there's plenty of precision. Your son is going to college next fall and the cost will be $45,000. This is short and precise.

But that same goal seventeen years ago was far more nebulous. You needed to plan for college, but was the goal a two-year associates degree or a program that terminated with an MBA, law degree, or medical degree? The uncertainty didn't mean you didn't need to plan and make choices. It meant you needed to make flexible and durable plans.

The same holds for each goal. Take retirement or financial independence, the dominant goal for most of us. We can't really know when it will be achieved or mandated. Health, economic, or technological change could greatly accelerate or perhaps delay your retirement. Twenty years ago, could we really have predicted the world in which we find ourselves today? For some, the answer is yes. For many, it's heck no.

To extend the basic metaphor, it's as much about financing the journey as arriving at the destination. And although I am a financial planner, I believe it's more about resilience than actual planning. A bit of Yiddish wisdom translates, "Man plans, God laughs." This is why our plans must be revisited and adjusted frequently. They must also be protected. Just as I used to purchase traveler's checks to secure my trips' financing, so too must we use insurance smartly to make sure that if we hit life's bumps, our plans can simply be adjusted, not completely discarded. We can't know precisely how much money we'll need, as unlike the road trip we can't calculate the miles to be traveled with any precision. If I make it to 90, I will need far more than if my time comes at 55 or 75. The prices you'll pay and even the goods and services you will purchase in the distant future can only be estimated today. It's not akin to the dinner at Denny's I knew I'd find off the interstate on my trips. Back then, I knew the price down to the dollar. It was knowable.

So, while it's not all knowable, it is doable. More to the point, your financial life will happen whether your plan for it or not. Dr. Stephen Covey noted in his bestseller *The 7 Habits of Highly Successful People* that all great things in life are created twice, first conceptually and then in reality. He also noted that in all areas of our lives, we are working on a plan. The only question is, whose plan? When it comes to financing your life, it should be yours. I hope this book helps make that so.

ACKNOWLEDGMENTS

"If you see a turtle on a fencepost," so goes the country saying, "you know it had help getting there." A personal finance book is not quite the feat of a turtle on a post, but it too requires a lot of help. I've been lucky to have had such help my entire life, from the construction crews of my youth who taught me what hard work and teamwork is; to my future brother-in-law Thane Christopher who helped me write my first newspaper columns for the *UW Daily*; to Sally C. Pipes and Virginia Postrel, my professional mentors who put up with my rough edges and worked diligently make up for all the English classes I never attended.

This book would not be possible without real-world instruction my clients provide each day. Thank you for placing your trust in me and my team. Serving you is my professional mission and I love what I do and do what I love. Speaking of my team, this book's creation spans many critical teammates, from Alisa Olsen, Blair Kasemann, Mr. Buckles and Lauren Humphrey in the early years to my current crew of Sarah Rizk, Gorete Braga, Tom Melfi, and Steve Cohen. Thank you for the assistance you provide our clients.

Success appears at the confluence of many factors, often with luck being one of the greatest contributors. I was lucky the day I met Paul Blanco and he recruited me to create my financial planning practice at Barnum Financial Group, a truly special place. This book would have never made it to its publisher without the efforts of Barnum's Jyoti Naik and Lorraine Caggiano. Thank you for your diligence. I can't think of a better pair than you to have my back and look out for our clients' interests.

If any errors escaped any of these watchful eyes, I am, of course, fully responsible.

ABOUT THE AUTHOR

MICHAEL LYNCH is a Certified Financial Planner with nearly twenty years of experience working with American families to craft plans that fund their dreams, educate their children, and finance their retirement.

Michael has contributed to the *Wall Street Journal* and *Investor's Business Daily*, and has hosted *Smart Money Radio* for a decade. He's served as an adjunct faculty member at Fairfield University and currently teaches financial planning to employees of corporations like Madison Square Garden and Yale New Haven Health Systems. Michael is a five-time Financial Planner of the Year for MetLife and a 2019 inductee to the Barnum Financial Group Hall of Fame. You can enjoy his latest articles and videos at www.michaelwlynch.com.

CPSIA information can be obtained
at www.ICGtesting.com
Printed in the USA
FSHW010027161020

9 781544 515526